HANDMADE BOOKS
FOR A HEALTHY PLANET

Sixteen Earth-Friendly Projects
From Around The World

Susan Kapuscinski Gaylord

makingbooks.com

To my husband and children, Charlie, Brendan and Kendra, my companions on the journey

Some of the material in this book is based on the author's previous work, *Multicultural Books To Make And Share*.

Illustrations: Susan Kapuscinski Gaylord
Cover design: Brendan Gaylord
Editorial Assistance: Lucia Greene

ISBN: 978-0-9842319-0-4

Library of Congress Catalog Number: 2010903022

Every effort has been made to ensure that all the information in this book, which is based on the author's experience, is correct. However, the author and the publisher take no responsibility for any harm which might be caused by the use or misuse of any materials or procedures mentioned in this book, nor is any condition or warranty implied.

makingbooks.com
Box 852
Newburyport, Massachusetts 01950

Printed and Bound in the United States of America

Table of Contents

Handmade Books for a Healthy Planet is about three things: making and creating books, connecting with cultures across the globe by exploring different forms of books, and using recycled materials to conserve resources and learn to look at the things we discard in a fresh way. It is also the expression of a big part of the last twenty years of my life. I began making books when my first child was two, two years after the life-changing year that brought the birth of my son and the death of my mother. Making books gave me a place to both celebrate and grieve.

I started by making books about the closest things around me, my children and my memories. Over the years, I have expanded to the world at large: the clouds in the sky, the leaves in the trees, events in history. Making books gives me a way of looking both inward and outward. It has made me more creative and more curious. It has given me a quiet center in this ever-more-quickly-moving world. I hope that making handmade books will do the same for you.

in good spirit

Susan

 # About this Book

Handmade Books for A Healthy Planet teaches you how to make sixteen handmade books, four from each of four areas of the world: Africa, the Americas, Asia, and Europe. Each section begins with a history of the book in that part of the world. All of the books are based on traditional forms and are arranged in order of difficulty. They take me between ten minutes and a half-hour to construct, but may take longer with young children or a large group. Adding the content is done after the book is made and can take as long as you want.

Each project opens with a photograph of books I made to show the variety of materials you can use, encouraging you to experiment. The cultural/historical inspiration for the book is followed by a description of the project and a list of things you'll need. The tools are the simplest and the materials are mostly recycled.

Making the book has step-by-step instructions for the construction of the book. I have made them as clear and detailed as possible. If you are teaching others, I find it is always best to demonstrate the steps by making a book of your own.

Fill the book appears when the introductory explanation doesn't give you all the information you need to complete the book. There are charts to help you write runes and Roman numerals, information on writing haiku, and adinkra symbols from Africa to copy and use.

Vary the Book suggests ways to vary the construction of the book as well as additional ideas for content.

Books to Read gives a sampling of picture books and folktale collections that can be read as an accompaniment. Some books have very specific connections and directly echo the theme of the projects. Others are related only in that they are a story from or about that particular culture. A brief description of each book is included along with publication information.

Recycled/Repurposed/Upcycled

While I use the word recycled to describe the materials we use, repurposed or upcycled might be better words. The *Oxford American Dictionary* defines recycle as "return (material) to a previous stage of a cyclic process, esp. convert (waste) to a reusable material." Recycling paper gives us more paper, recycling glass makes glass. When we make books from discarded materials, we are making something new. We can use the term repurpose because we are taking something (a cereal box or a grocery bag) and using it for another purpose. But the term I like the best is upcycle which was coined by William McDonough and Michael Braungart, authors of *Cradle to Cradle: Remaking the Way We Make Things*. Wikipedia defines it like this: "Upcycling is the practice of taking something that is disposable and transforming it into something of greater use and value." McDonough and Braungart point out the recycling is not an even exchange. The paper that gets recycled does not make paper of equal quality without the addition of other materials and the use of energy. When we reuse paper to make a book, we are using it in its entirety. The energy we use is only our own and what we create has new meaning and greater value.

Paper

The main ingredient in making books is paper, heavier for the covers and lighter for the pages. The books in *Handmade Books for a Healthy Planet* use three main kinds:

Brown paper grocery bags: Front and back panels and occasionally the side panels.

Cereal boxes: Front and back panels without the flaps on the top and bottom and occasionally the side panels. I use the term cereal boxes in the directions but you can also use cracker boxes, waffle boxes, leftover file folders, anything that is sturdy but will fold.

Used US Letter/A4 paper with writing on one side only.

The project directions do not specify sizes but rather ask for shapes. Rectangular paper can be the front or back panel of a grocery bag, US Letter/A4 recycled paper, or whatever you have available. Long narrow paper is used for folded accordion books. It can be made by folding US Letter/A4 paper in half the long way or by cutting a front or back grocery panel in half the long way. Paper that has writing on one side can be folded to hide the writing on the inside of the fold or two pieces can be glued together with the writing sides facing each other to form one sheet of paper that is blank on both sides. Paper with writing and designs can also be used for books. The writing is done on separate pieces of paper and glued onto the pages. I often use newspapers, catalog pages, and leftover wrapping paper.

For Sewing and Tying

Yarn: Yarn is best for books that use knots to hold them together. Ribbon tends to be too slippery to hold. I save scraps of yarn and string, but also keep a skein or two of purchased yarn on hand. I prefer variegated yarns which are readily available.

Ribbon: I like to use ribbon for ties on accordion books. I save it from gift packages, both the curling kind and flat ribbon. I also buy it at craft and sewing stores. If you've converted to DVDs, you can reuse tape from old videos. I find it easier to get the tape out if I take the case apart with a small Phillips head screwdriver. If you are threading ribbon through holes, it is best to cut the ends on the diagonal.

Thread for sewing: The thread should be fairly thick and strong. I usually use crochet cotton, but dental floss and carpet thread also work well. Embroidery floss comes in great colors but you need to be careful when threading the needle because of the separate strands.

Cutting Yarn, Ribbon, and Thread: The directions use either the book or your fingers, hands, and arms—such as yarn twice the length of the page or one arm-length long—as measuring guides. This works great if you are working alone or in a small group. If you are working with a large group, it's helpful to have the yarn already cut to size.

Handmade Books for a Healthy Planet/ ©2010 Susan Kapuscinski Gaylord /makingbooks.com

To save time cutting, I use strips of heavy corrugated cardboard about one hand-width wide as measuring guides. The short measure is 12"/30cm and the long measure is 18"/46cm. I wrap the yarn or ribbon around the cardboard. For yarn the length of the cardboard, I cut it at both ends, yielding 12"/30cm and 18"/46cm lengths. For yarn twice the length of the cardboard, I cut it at one end only for lengths 24"/60cm and 36"/92cm.

Elastics: I save them from vegetables and the newspaper delivery.

Twist ties: I save them from bread and other plastic bags.

Pony Beads: These plastic beads have large holes so they work well for stringing with yarn. I buy them at craft stores. I store them in plastic containers and pour them into applesauce or other small containers when making books with a group.

Other Beads, Buttons, and Shells: I always look at necklaces and bracelets at yard sales and rummage sales and buy ones with interesting beads. I've also purchased plant holders made from shells. I take them apart when I get home and store the beads and shells in plastic containers, jars, or resealable plastic bags.

Plastic bread closures: They can be used instead of beads.

Tubes and Cylinders: The two scroll projects use tubes and plastic containers. In the *Name Scroll*, the scroll is mounted on a paper tube. You can also use a spent glue stick. The *Wish Scroll* uses a plastic container as a case for the scroll. I have used film containers, the tops of some glue sticks, and plastic lids from things like vinegar and soy sauce. Film is being used less and less but you still may be able to get containers at places that print photos on the premises.

Popsicle Sticks: I wash and save them for the *Slat Book*.

Catalogs: Always use scrap paper when you glue. Catalog pages are perfect for this. They can also be sources of imagery for your books.

Collage Box: The pride and joy of my bookmaking materials is my collage box. I cut or tear any interesting colored paper that comes my way—wrapping paper from gifts, paper bags, old calendars, security envelopes with patterns inside, can labels, maps, etc.—into small squares and keep them in a box. I find that the smaller size wastes less paper and seems to stimulate creativity in a way that large pieces of paper don't.

Organizing Your Materials

It's good to have some materials on hand so you are ready to make books when inspiration strikes or you have a few spare moments. You shouldn't feel obligated to save so many things that you become overwhelmed. I like to have 4 to 6 grocery bags and the same amount of cereal boxes on hand. The boxes can be flattened for easier storage. To keep the edges from bending, I store used paper with writing on one side in a box that is close to the size of the paper. Since I work at home, I produce quantities of paper but if you don't, collect used paper at work or ask family and friends to do so. Labeled shoe boxes are good for yarn, ribbon and miscellaneous materials. I have a small jar in the kitchen that I use to save bread closures, twist ties and elastics. When the jar is full, I sort the items and put them with my bookmaking materials.

 # Measuring Guide

Instead of rulers, use fingers, hands, and arms to measure.

THUMB-END

THUMB-LENGTH

THUMB-WIDTH

INDEX FINGER-LENGTH

HAND-WIDTH

HAND-LENGTH

ARM-LENGTH

You probably already have the tools you need but if you can, you might want to get a separate set and store them in a box just for bookmaking so that they are easy to find. There is nothing to put you off starting a project like having to spend fifteen minutes looking for that pair of scissors you used not that long ago. If you want to work together as a group, whether it be as a family or in a class, you might want to have a set of tools for each person. I have listed only the tools used for making the books. Use your choice of markers, colored pencils, or crayons to fill in the books. I tend to avoid paint and other wet media to keep clean-up to a minimum but you should feel free to use whatever you please.

Scissors: There's quite a bit of cutting involved when using recycled materials. Scissors that cut well are a big help. For children, I like the Fiskars brand scissors. I prefer the pointed ones, which are still not too pointy. If you don't have scissors, you can always tear the paper instead.

Hole Punch: A hole punch is used for several of the projects. If you don't have one, the pointy end of a pair of scissors can be poked through the paper and twisted to make the hole. This task is best saved for adults.

Glue: I love glue sticks. They are neater than white glue and because there is no moisture in the glue, the paper will dry flat. I prefer colored glue sticks. They spread on colored so you can see where the glue is but dry clear. My favorite is UHU brand. Some people feel that the glue dries too quickly. I like them because you can reposition the pieces if you need to.

If you don't have glue sticks, you can use homemade flour paste or wall paper paste and a brush. The paper will be much more likely to buckle from the moisture so it is important to press the book under some heavy books or other weight overnight or until dry.

Recipe for Cooked Flour Paste
1 part flour   1 part cold water   2 parts boiling water

I usually make it with one part equaling ½ cup

Put the flour in a pan or a double boiler. Add the cold water gradually, stirring until all lumps are removed. A whisk works well. Slowly add the boiling water and cook the mixture 3-4 minutes, stirring constantly. Cover it and let it cool. If you use a microwave, you only have to cook the mixture 1–2 minutes and you don't need to stir. It will expand quite a bit as it cooks so use a large cooking container. Store the unused paste in a covered container in the refrigerator, where it should keep for at least two weeks and sometimes much longer.

Scrap Paper: Any project with gluing also needs scrap paper. This protects the table surface and keeps your book from getting covered with glue. I use pages from catalogs, junk mail, and paper from the recycle bin that has writing on both sides.

Sewing Kit: There are lots of small bits and pieces when you sew books together. I make sewing kits from Altoid tins or resealable plastic bags which contain:

- 1 size 16 tapestry needle (I prefer tapestry needles because they have a dull point. The large eye of the size 16 makes it easy to thread which is good for young children and old eyes.)

- 2 spring-type clothespins (or paper clips)

- 1 small pencil (for marking the holes)

- 1 nail (to make holes for the *Book of Haiku* binding)

- 1 push pin (to make holes for the *Book of Hours* binding)

- 1 small piece of cardboard (to protect the table when making holes for the *Book of Hours* binding)

Folding

Folding is probably used in more of the books than any other technique. I'm not looking for perfection, but I do like the folding to be done as carefully as possible. It works best if you use both hands when folding. Once you've brought the corners together, one hand (the holding hand) holds the paper in place. The other hand (the folding hand) flattens the paper and makes the crease.

1. Bring one side of the paper to the other and line the corners up. Some kindergarten and preschool teachers tell the kids to make the corners kiss.

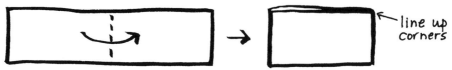

line up corners

2. Use one hand to hold the paper in place.

hold paper in place

3. Flatten the fold by pressing with your folding hand. Then run the side of your thumb along the fold to make the crease. You can add some extra crispness to the fold by going over it with the side of a pair of scissors or a glue stick (with the cap on). I find it especially helpful when I am using a grocery bag or something that already has some creases in it. It is easier to tell the folds I made from the ones that are already there.

Gluing

Three Basic Rules of Gluing:

1. Put glue on the smaller of the two pieces that are being attached.

2. Use scrap paper. Using scrap paper keeps you from making a mess of the table as well as your book.

3. Apply pressure after gluing to help the glue adhere.

The Process:

Place the paper to be glued on the scrap paper. Cover the entire surface with a thin coat of glue. Start in the middle and work toward the edges. I usually do stripes up and then stripes down. Go over the edges and onto the scrap paper.

After the paper is covered with glue, remove the scrap paper and fold it in half with the glue on the inside so nothing will stick to it.

Carefully position the glued piece. When it is in the proper place, rub it with your hand to help the glue adhere. If you make a mistake and position the glued piece improperly, you can often correct it if you work quickly before the glue has dried and you have pressed it.

If you can, press the glued books under weight (heavy books will do) for several hours or overnight. If you have used wet paste and a brush, you must press the books because the moisture will cause the paper to buckle. Wrap the books in waxed paper and press until dry.

Tying Knots

All of the knots used are double knots. The simplest ones are just two knots, tied one after the other. In a few of the projects, a bead is tied to the end of a piece of yarn.

    1. Put the yarn through the hole in the bead.
    2. Tie a knot around the bead so that the bead is inside the knot.
    3. Tighten the knot around the bead.
    4. Tie a second knot. Tug on the bead to tighten the knot.

Square knots, which are more secure, are a kind of double knot. You may remember square knots from Girl or Boy Scouts, "right over left, left over right." If you don't know how to make a square knot, you can learn from the following directions or not worry about it (my recommendation) and just tie a double knot.

Each hand holds one end of the cord. For the first knot, the cord that is in your right hand goes on top of the cord that is in your left hand (right over left). For the second knot, the cord that is in your left hand goes on top of the cord that is in your right hand (left over right). Pull to tighten.

Threading Yarn Through Holes

Several of the books require you to thread yarn through holes. If you are not careful, the yarn can unravel and make a mess. I have two solutions:

For younger children, prepare the end of the yarn ahead of time. Dip the end in white glue and let it dry or put a small piece of tape around the end and twist it so it is like a shoelace. The yarn will also be easier to thread.

For everyone else: Instead of pushing the end of the yarn through the hole, fold the end of the yarn down to make a small loop and push the loop through the hole.

Make a loop at end of yarn before inserting in hole

Doing the Writing

I approach bookmaking pretty casually. I like to keep it fun and usually don't do a lot of planning ahead. I don't worry about writing in a straight line but if you do, there are some line guides available online. If you're concerned about errors, you can do the writing on another piece of paper, check it for spelling and grammar and then copy it into the book. You may find it helpful to work with paper the same size as the book pages. You can also write directly in the book with pencil, then check it and go over your writing with marker. If you do make a mistake in the book, don't worry about it. Even the beautiful illuminated manuscripts made by medieval monks had mistakes. The easiest way to fix it is to glue a piece of paper on top of your mistake. You can cover a whole page or section or just a word or two.

 What is a Book?

Books are first and foremost about communication: recording information, preserving memories, and expressing feelings. The earliest communication was what we call oral tradition: people telling stories and singing songs to preserve knowledge. One person would teach another who would teach another. There always needed to be direct contact, face to face, mouth to ear, for the transfer of information. Books extend communication across time and space. I can create a book here and you can read it there days, weeks, months, years later. I have defined the handmade book very broadly in *Handmade Books for a Healthy Planet*. There are books that do not fit our vision of what a book looks like but can be described by this definition: a handmade article of portable communication.

The first books were made from available materials: clay, bark, leaves, wood, leather and cloth. Later, materials were developed specifically for the making of books: papyrus, parchment and paper. Different materials led to the development of different forms of books. Cloth and papyrus were rolled into scrolls, strips of wood were tied together, and parchment and then paper was folded and sewn. Until relatively recently in the history of the book, all books were handmade. The preparation of the pages, the folding, sewing, or tying, the writing and illustration were all done by hand. To get a copy of a book, one truly had to copy it, word by word, page by page.

In *Handmade Books for a Healthy Planet*, we are again making books by hand. We are following the spirit of the early bookmakers and adapting our books to use the materials that we have at hand. We are replacing palm leaves with recycled cereal boxes, wood and bamboo slats with popsicle sticks, and papyrus with grocery bags.

AFRICA

The large continent of Africa with its diverse climates and populations has strong written and oral traditions. One of the earliest book forms, the papyrus scroll, came from ancient Egypt. Christianity in the fourth century and Islam in the seventh century brought additional influences. Africa's oral tradition is often enhanced and aided by a variety of storytelling devices and memory aids of cloth, wood and beads.

The scrolls of ancient Egypt and Nubia were made of papyrus, a plant that grows along the Nile River. The stems were cut into thin strips. The strips were laid on top of each other in two layers, one horizontal and one vertical. They were then pressed until they meshed together to form a paper-like substance. Papyrus was usually made in pieces about the size of US Legal paper that were glued together and rolled to form a scroll. The scroll was used for government and business records, as well as religious writings, literature and science books. One of the most common books was *The Book of the Dead* which contained descriptions of the afterlife and was buried with the dead. The writing, done with a reed and ink made from carbon, was called hieroglyphics or picture writing. Papyrus scrolls were in use from about 3,000 BCE until the 4th century CE. Their influence was widespread in the ancient world, including classical Greece and Rome.

The Copts of Egypt converted to Christianity in the second century. They made books of folded sheets of papyrus sewn together along the fold. Thick covers of pressed papyrus, rather like heavy cardboard, were covered with leather and decorated. Their particular way of sewing the book together, with the thread exposed along the spine, is still used today by bookbinders and called the Coptic binding.

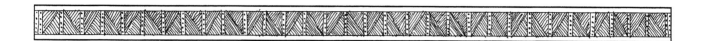

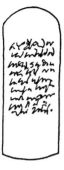 Islam was the other major influence on book production in Africa. Scrolls were widely used in all of Islamic Africa from the seventh century. Timbuktu in Mali was a center of learning in the fourteenth century where important books were written and copied. In West Africa, the Koran is taught to students in Arabic by means of wooden boards. Some boards have the texts written on them. Others are for students to practice writing. The writing is done with charcoal and the board is washed clean after using. The boards start out a light color and darken with use. In Ethiopia, talismanic scrolls were made and worn as protection and prayer.

In Africa, there is a strong tradition of storytelling on cloth. The court of Dahomey in Benin in western Africa had appliqué cloths made to commemorate their lives and important events. In Ghana, adinkra cloths are made by printing fabric with stamps carved from gourds. The patterns are chosen from a set of symbols, each with its own special meaning. The cloths were originally made as mourning cloths but have expanded to other uses.

 Machine printed cloths played an important part in the independence movements in Africa in the 1960s. They promoted national identity, democracy and literacy. They are still made and worn today with public health and political messages.

There are other examples of communication devices from different parts of Africa. Young Zulu women send messages to their boyfriends and husbands through pieces of handmade beadwork. In Zaire, the Luba make Lukasa, decorated boards which pass on the mythology and morals of the secret society to initiates.

NAME SCROLL

EGYPT

From back to front: (1) Scroll of grocery bag mounted on spent glue stick. Images cut from magazines and catalogs. Yarn tie with bread closures on ends. (2) Scroll of grocery bag mounted on half toilet paper tube. Images drawn with marker. Yarn tie with bread closures on ends. (3) Rolled grocery bag/toilet paper scroll with curling ribbon tie. (4) Scrolls (open and closed) on recycled copy paper glued to catalog pages mounted on empty thread spools. Name images drawn with black marker, swirls added around images and then images colored in. Ties cut from plastic rice cake bags.

The earliest writing was in the form of picture symbols, or pictographs. As time went on, the pictures came to represent sounds. Because the pictures were time consuming to draw, they slowly changed into abstract symbols representing sounds — alphabets. We write with what is called the Roman alphabet because the letters were used in ancient Rome. The Roman alphabet had its beginning in hieroglyphs, the picture writing of ancient Egypt.

The *Name Scroll* spells out your name using pictures that start with the letters. My name is Susan and my scroll has: sun, umbrella, sun, apple and the number nine. You can draw the pictures or cut them out of magazines and catalogs. A tie at the end slips over the scroll to hold it closed.

With young children, it is helpful to cut the scroll strips ahead. You can also staple the scroll strip to the toilet paper tube instead of gluing to save time.

You'll Need:

- 1 paper tube (I used a toilet paper tube cut in half) or spent glue stick

- Front or back panel of grocery bag or used paper with writing on one side only

- 1 piece of yarn or ribbon, 4 times the height of the cut tube or Short Measure x 1 (See page 9.)

- Scissors

- Pencil

- Glue stick and scrap paper

Development of Alphabet

EGYPTIAN HIEROGLYPHS	TRANSITIONAL STAGES	ROMAN ALPHABET
OX	→	→ A	A
HOUSE	→	→	B
DOOR	→	→	D
WATER	→	→	M
FISH	→	→	N
EYE	→	→	O

1. Cut the scroll paper:

a. Place the bag panel or paper in front of you so that it is taller than wide. Place the tube on the bottom corner and make a pencil mark next to it. You may want to add more lines up the paper to make it easier to keep a straight line when cutting. Starting at the line, cut a strip of paper.

b. Using the cut strip as a guide, cut a second strip of scroll paper. If your name is long, cut a third piece.

2. Glue the scroll paper to the tube:

a. Place the tube on the end of one of the scroll strips. If the paper has writing on it, it should be not be showing. Roll the tube so that the paper covers the tube and make a pencil mark after the tube.

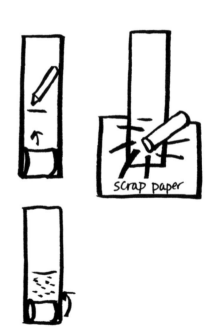

b. Using scrap paper, put glue on the scroll strip from the pencil mark to the end. If it has writing on one side, put the glue on the side without the writing.

c. Place the tube on the edge of the scroll strip with the glue. Roll the tube pressing it into the paper. Put your thumbs inside the tube and rub the outside with firm pressure to help the paper adhere to the tube.

3. Make the scroll strip longer:

Using scrap paper, apply a thumb-width wide stripe of glue on the end of the scroll strip and place the next piece on top with the writing side down. Apply pressure to help the glue adhere.

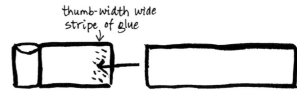

4. Draw the sound pictures that spell out your name.

5. Fold a tab at the end and make a hole:

a. Place your hand next to the last picture and make a pencil mark on the other side of your hand. Using the pencil mark as a guide, cut off any extra paper.

b. Fold a tab one thumb-width wide at the end of the scroll strip.

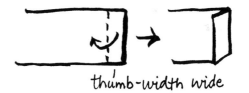

c. Fold that tab over to make a double thick tab.

d. Punch a hole in the center of the tab.

6. Attach a tie:

a. Fold the yarn in half.

b. Put the loop at the center of the folded yarn through the hole. Pull the loop from the back of the hole and open it up. Put the ends of the yarn through the loop and pull to tighten.

c. Roll up the scroll. Wrap one end of yarn around the scroll to one side and the other end around to the other side. Halfway around the scroll, tie the two strands together in a double knot. You have now made a loop of yarn that can be placed around the scroll to hold it closed and lifted off to open it.

Handmade Books for a Healthy Planet/ ©2010 Susan Kapuscinski Gaylord /makingbooks.com

 # Vary the Book

Draw designs around the sound pictures with black marker. Color in the sound pictures but not the designs.

Tie beads, buttons or bread closures on the ends of the yarn.

Make a group scroll for a family or class. Use a paper towel tube. Write the names in sound pictures in vertical columns. Glue a photograph or draw a picture next to each name.

 # Read a Book

The Day of Ahmed's Secret, Florence Parry Heide and Judith Heide Gilliland. New York: Lothrop, Lee, and Shepard, 1990. Ahmed, a young boy in contemporary Egypt, spends his day delivering water. The sights and sounds of Cairo are vividly described. At the end of the day, he reveals his secret: he has learned to write his name.

The Shipwrecked Sailor: An Egyptian Tale with Hieroglyphs, Tamara Bower. New York: Atheneum Books for Young Readers, 2000. Based on a story found in an ancient papyrus scroll, this story tells of a shipwreck on the island of the soul and a happy homecoming. One line on each page has been translated into hieroglyphs. The illustrations were inspired by papyrus scrolls.

The Egyptian Cinderella, Shirley Climo. New York: Crowell, 1989. Set in Egypt in the sixth century BCE, this Cinderella is Rhodopes, a slave girl who is chosen by the pharaoh to be queen.

WISH SCROLL

ETHIOPIA

Left (1): Scroll case of rice vinegar cap covered with grocery bag paper. Curling ribbon saved from gifts for hanger. Scroll of grocery bag paper. / Right Front (2): Scroll case of top of glue stick covered with grocery bag paper. Yarn hanger. / Right Back (3): Scroll case made from film container decorated with paper from the collage box. Hanger made from used videotape. Buttons tied onto videotape with thread.

Small scrolls that are placed in cases and worn for protection and prayer are made in Ethiopia. The cases are metal or leather and worn around the neck or tied to a belt. They contain prayers, cures or talismans to ward off evil. The ones for healing are made by religious figures called dabtaras who make scrolls from goatskin that are the exact height of the person to be cured.

Make your own wish scroll. Two ideas for starting are: "I wish. . ." or "May there be. . ." The wishes can be imaginary: "I wish I could sail in a sea of stars."; for something you want: "I wish I had a new computer game."; or for the world: "May there be peace in the world and in our hearts."

You'll Need:

- 1 small cylindrical container
- Side, front or back panel of grocery bag or used paper with writing on one side only for scroll
- Paper to cover container (grocery bag, catalog page, paper)
- 1 piece of thick thread, yarn or ribbon, 1 arm-length or Long Measure x 2 (See page 9.)
- Tape
- Scissors
- Pencil

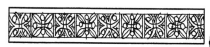 

1. Cut the paper for the scroll:

a. Place the paper in front of you so that it is taller than wide. Place the container on the corner and make a pencil mark slightly taller than the container. Add more lines up the paper to make it easier to keep a straight line when cutting.

pencil mark a little taller than container

b. Cut the scroll strip. If you are planning on a long wish, you may want to cut a second strip.

cut scroll strip

2. Attach the yarn to the container:

a. Place one end of the yarn on one side of the container near the top and tape it down. Tape the other end on the opposite side. You may find it helpful to have a partner assist you by holding the yarn while you tape.

tape

b. Put a longer piece of tape all around the container for a stronger hold.

tape

3. Cover the container:

a. Using leftover grocery bag or recycled paper, cut a piece of paper that is slightly shorter than the height of the container and long enough to wrap around.

b. Place the paper on a piece of scrap paper with the side you want to show face down and cover the entire surface with glue.

c. Set the container on the paper and carefully roll so that the paper adheres to the container.

d. Rub the paper to help the glue adhere.

4. Roll the scroll strip and place in container.

5. Attach decorative ties (optional).

Wrap a hand-length of yarn or thick thread around the hanger on each side of the container and tie a double knot. You may find it helpful to have a partner assist you. Add beads, buttons and/or bread closures to the ends for decoration.

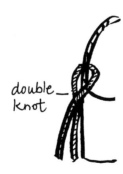

double knot

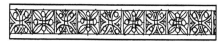 ## Vary the Book

Make an "I Have a Dream" scroll for Martin Luther King Day. Write your dreams for our society and our world on your scroll.

Make a scroll for Earth Day with a wish for the health of the planet.

Celebrate holidays with gift scrolls. Write wishes for Mother's Day, Father's Day or birthdays. Make an "I am thankful" scroll for Thanksgiving.

One of the original purposes of the scrolls was to write out cures. Make a get well scroll for a sick friend.

 ## Read a Book

The Lion's Whiskers: An Ethiopian Folktale, Nancy Raines Day, illustrated by Ann Grifalconi. New York: Scholastic, Inc., 1995. Trying to form a bond with her stepson who misses his mother who has died, Fanaye learns patience from the task assigned by the medicine man: bring him three whiskers from the chin of the fierce old lion. The book is illustrated with collages of textured materials and colored papers.

Pulling the Lion's Tale, Jane Kurtz, illustrated by Floyd Cooper. New York: Simon & Schuster Books for Young Readers, 1995. Using the plot from the traditional tale of the Lion's Whiskers, Jane Kurtz tells of a young girl learning patience as she gets to know her new stepmother. The warm illustrations complement the story of inner growth and give a view of the life of an Ethiopian child.

The Miracle Child: A Story from Ethiopia, Elizabeth Laird with Abba Aregawi Wolde Gabriel. New York: Holt, Rinehart and Winston, 1985. Ethiopia is one of the oldest Christian countries in the world. *The Miracle Child* tells the dramatic story of the well-loved Ethiopian saint, St. Tekla Haymanot. It is illustrated with vibrant paintings from an eighteenth century illuminated manuscript.

ZULU BEADWORK

SOUTH AFRICA

Left: Grid colored in with markers and mounted on cereal box. Yarn ties. / Right: Grid colored in with dots using colored pencils and mounted on grocery bag. Yarn ties.

Zulu girls and women sew small colored glass seed beads into neckbands for their boyfriends and husbands. The beadwork is designed to send a message. Colors and shapes stand for particular emotions and thoughts. Some express positive emotions of love and happiness, others negative emotions of jealousy and loneliness. Zulu women also make beadwork for sale. The small pieces mounted on large safety pins are called Zulu Love Tokens.

Make a paper beadwork neckband with the grid on page 36. Use the chart to assign meanings to different colors and shapes. Decide what you want your neckband to express and fill in the grid either by coloring in the squares or filling them with dots.

You'll Need:

- Beadwork grid on page 36

- 1 cereal box side panel
  or grocery bag side panel
  or two pieces of paper glued together

- 2 pieces of yarn,
  twice the length of the band
  or Short Measure x 2 (See page 9.)

- Glue stick and scrap paper

- Scissors

- Hole Punch

1. Attach the neckband grid to the panel:

a. Cut out the grid on the following page. Place the grid face down on scrap paper and apply glue to the back of the grid. Remember to cover the entire surface. Center the grid in the middle of the panel. Smooth with your hand to help the glue adhere.

b. Trim the two sides leaving about a thumb-length of panel on either side of the grid.

c. Trim the top and bottom close to the grid.

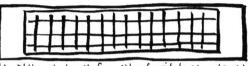

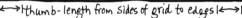

thumb-length from sides of grid to edges

d. On each side, center the punch from top to bottom, push the punch in as far as it will go, and punch a hole.

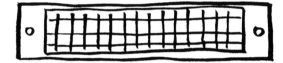

2. Attach the ties:

a. Fold one piece of yarn in half. Put the loop at the center of the folded yarn through the hole, starting from the front of the neckband. Pull the loop from the back of the hole and open it up. Put the ends of the yarn through the loop and pull to tighten.

b. Do the same thing on the other side.

I suggest making two copies of this page. Use one copy to assign meanings to colors and shapes and work out the design. Use the other copy for your finished neckband. If you use washable markers, make sure one color is dry before adding the next.

Colors   ## Shapes

Blue ——————————   X ——————————

Red ——————————   Triangle ——————————

Yellow ——————————   Diamond ——————————

Black ——————————   Square ——————————

Green ——————————   Zig Zag Line ——————————

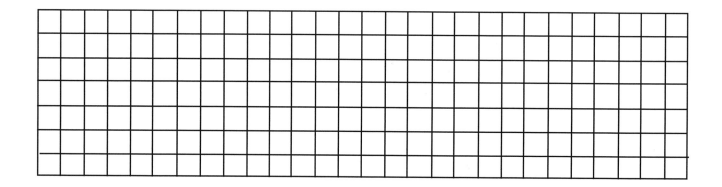

 # Vary the Book

Use graph paper with eight squares to an inch (the grid provided is four squares to the inch) and fine markers for a more detailed look.

A neckband is a great gift for Mother's Day, Father's Day, Kwanzaa, or a birthday. Write the meaning of the colors and shapes on the back so that the recipient can decode the message.

Punch circles from colored paper with a hole punch. Glue them into the grid. A simpler method (but not recycled) is to use the small round color coding dots available in office supply stores.

 # Read a Book

Shaka, King of the Zulus, Diane Stanley and Peter Vennema. New York: Morrow Jr. Books, 1988. This is the story of Shaka and his journey from outcast to king and fierce, innovative war leader. Drawings of beadwork run throughout the book as border elements and complement the rich illustrations.

Mufaro's Beautiful Daughters: An African Tale, John Steptoe. New York: Lothrop, Lee & Shephard, 1987. Inspired by a Zimbabwean folktale, John Steptoe's beautifully illustrated and told story of two beautiful sisters, one kind and one mean, shows the triumph of goodness.

ADINKRA CLOTH

GHANA

Left: Two pieces of colored paper with writing on one side glued together for background. Symbols cut from pages from a catalog. / Right: Back panel of grocery bag cut in half for background. Symbols traced and colored in with black marker.

Adinkra cloths from Ghana are covered with symbols that represent meanings. Most cloths are printed with stamps cut from a gourd (illustration on left) and a black dye called adinkra which means "farewell" in Twi, the language of the Akan people. The dye comes from a mixture made from the boiled bark of the badie tree and an iron-rich stone. Sometimes the cloths are made with sewn cloth symbols. First made as mourning cloths, adinkra cloths are often commissioned today by people embarking on a new venture, such as starting a business.

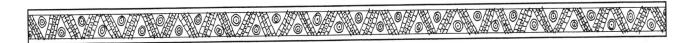

Your adinkra cloth will have six symbols. You can make a cloth for yourself, a friend or family member, a historical figure you admire or a favorite character in a book. You can use the traditional adinkra symbols on the following pages or design your own.

The patterns are a little tricky to cut so you might want to precut them for younger children. If you will use the patterns a lot, you can make them sturdier by printing them on cover stock or gluing them onto a cereal box panel.

You'll Need:

- 1 front or back panel of a grocery bag cut in half or 2 pieces of used paper glued together with the writing sides facing each other

- Small pieces of paper for the symbols

- Symbol patterns on pages 42 and 43

- Glue stick and scrap paper

- Scissors

- Pencil

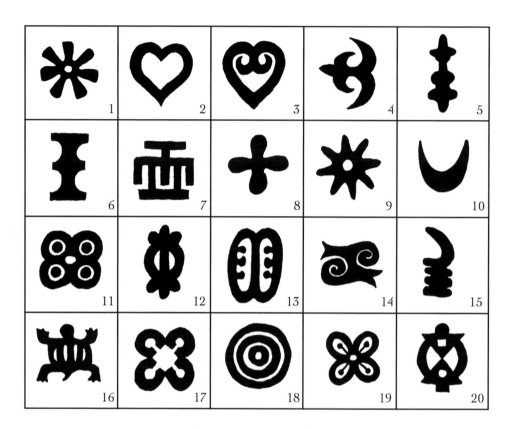

Adinkra Symbols

1. *Ananse ntontan*, spider's web. Symbol of wisdom, creativity and the complexities of life.

2. *Akoma*, heart. Symbol of goodwill, patience, fondness, faithfulness.

3. *Sankofa*, "Return and pick it up." Learn from or build on the past. Pick up what's good in the past to bring to the future.

4. *Akoko nan tia ne ba a enkum no,* "If a hen steps on its chick, the chick does not die." Symbol of mercy, protectiveness, discipline with patience.

5. *Okodee mmowere,* eagle's talons. Symbol of strength.

6. *Donno ntoasa,* drum. Symbol of merriment, alertness, skill with hands.

7. *Hwemudua,* measuring rod. Symbol of excellence, intolerance of imperfection.

8. *Tabono,* paddle for canoe. Symbol of strength, confidence, persistence.

9. *Nsoromma,* star. "Like the star, the child of the Supreme Being, I rest with God and so I do not depend on myself."

10. *Osram,* the moon. Symbol of faith, patience, understanding and determination.

11. *Ntesie or Matie masie,* "What I hear, I keep." Symbol of wisdom, knowledge, prudence.

12. *Wawa aba,* seeds of owawa tree. Symbol of hardiness, sticking to goals.

13. *Ese ne tekrema,* teeth and tongue. Symbol of friendliness and interdependence.

14. *Kwatakye atiko,* back of Kwatakye's head. Special hairstyle of captain of old Asante. Symbol of bravery and valor.

15. *Akoben,* war horn. Symbol of readiness to be called to arms.

16. *Denkyem,* crocodile. Symbol of adaptability.

17. *Agyinda wuru,* Agyin's gong. Agyin was a faithful servant to the King of Asante. Symbol of alertness and dutifulness.

18. *Adinkrahene,* king of the adinkra designs. Symbol of greatness, prudence, firmness and magnanimousness.

19. *Bese saka,* sack of cola nuts. Symbol of affluence, power, abundance, plenty, togetherness and unity

20. *Boa me na me mmoa wo,* "Help me and let me help you." Symbol of cooperation and interdependence.

Adinkra Patterns

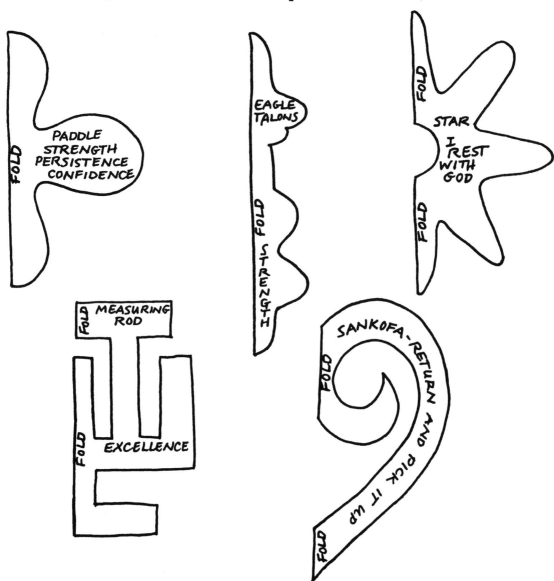

FOLD — PADDLE STRENGTH PERSISTENCE CONFIDENCE

EAGLE TALONS — FOLD STRENGTH

FOLD — STAR I REST WITH GOD — FOLD

FOLD MEASURING ROD — EXCELLENCE — FOLD

SANKOFA-RETURN AND PICK IT UP — FOLD — FOLD

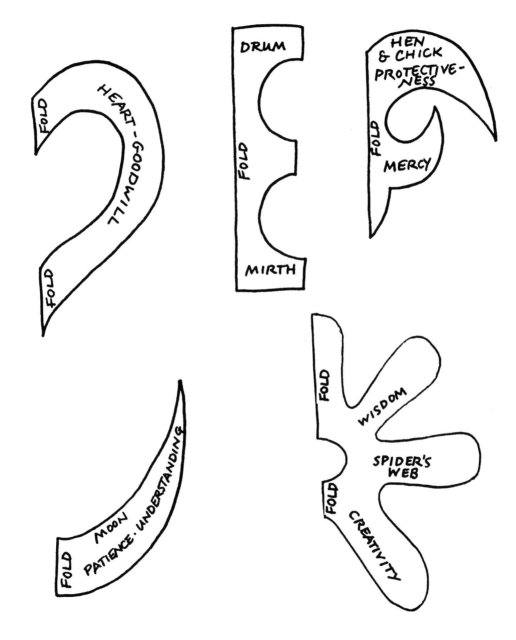

HEART ~ GOODWILL
FOLD
FOLD

DRUM
FOLD
MIRTH

HEN & CHICK PROTECTIVE-NESS
FOLD
MERCY

MOON PATIENCE · UNDERSTANDING
FOLD

WISDOM
FOLD
SPIDER'S WEB
FOLD
CREATIVITY

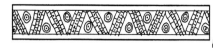 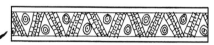
1. Make the symbols:

a. Copy and cut out the symbols on the preceding pages. You may want to glue them to a cereal box panel for durability.

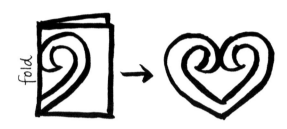

b. To make each symbol, fold a piece of paper in half with the side you want to show on the inside. Place the pattern on the paper so that the pattern fold indication is on the fold of the paper. You might find it helpful to paper clip the pattern to the paper. Trace the pattern and cut.

2. Prepare the paper:

a. As guides for the placement of the symbols, fold the paper in half so that it is long and skinny like a hot dog. You'll put a row of symbols above and a row below.

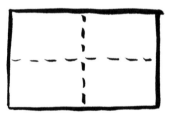

b. Open the paper and fold it half the other way, like a hamburger. This gives you a center line to help you evenly place the symbols from left to right.

3. Place and glue the symbols:

Using scrap paper, cover the back side of each symbol with glue. Place it on the "cloth" and smooth to help the glue adhere.

 # Vary the Book

Design your own symbols. The symbols on the cloth represent qualities and values that are important to the people of Ghana. What qualities and values are important to you, your family and your culture?

Use cookie cutters as patterns. Trace around the cookie cutter with a pencil and color in the shapes. Or trace around the cookie cutter on black or colored paper, cut out and glue. Assign meanings to the symbols.

Read a Book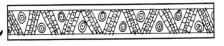

The Talking Cloth, Rhonda Mitchell. New York: Orchard Books, 1997. African-American Amber visits her Aunt Phoebe whose house is full of things Amber's father calls junk and her aunt calls her "collection of life." Amber's favorite is an adinkra cloth from Ghana. There are descriptions of the cloth and the meaning of some of the symbols. Amber imagines the cloths she would make for her family.

Anansi the Spider: A Tale from the Ashanti, adapted and illustrated by Gerald McDermott. New York: Holt, Rinehart and Winston, 1972. A graphically stunning retelling of the story of Anansi and his six sons who work together to save their father when he is in danger. The sons all have the same legs and heads and are distinguished from one another by the symbols that make up their bodies.

The Hat-Shaking Dance and Other Ashanti Tales from Ghana, Harold Courlander with Albert Kofi Prempeh. New York: Harcourt, Brace & World, Inc., 1957. Twenty-one Ashanti tales from Ghana, excellent for reading aloud, are featured in this book. Many are about Anansi, the spider, including "All Stories Are Anansi's."

AMERICAS

The history of the book in the Americas can be divided into two broad categories: books by native peoples and books brought by the Europeans.

The most developed indigenous book form was the codex of the Mayans and Aztecs of Mexico and Central America. These accordion books were made of deerskin or amatyl paper (amate in Spanish) which was formed by boiling strips of the inner bark of the fig tree and pounding them until they meshed together. The folded books, usually with wooden covers, were used for ritual calendars, tribute lists, genealogies and historical chronicles. The writing was done with pictures called glyphs which represented sounds as well as specific objects. Most of the books were destroyed by the Spanish. The oldest book still in existence, the Dresden Codex, dates from the twelfth century.

In South America, the Inca of Peru made quipu, which were knotted strings called remembering strings. Quipu were an important tool in the Inca empire which stretched from Ecuador to Chile. There were two types: those used for accounting, in which the knots recorded the production and distribution of crops and other goods as well as population counts, and those in which the knots represented words.

Handmade Books for a Healthy Planet/ ©2010 Susan Kapuscinski Gaylord /makingbooks.com

The native North American book traditions include a variety of pictographic work. The Ojibwa in Minnesota made birch bark scrolls to preserve the knowledge needed for the Midewiwin, or Medicine Dance. The Dakota made winter counts, which recorded their history on buffalo hides. Other Plains Indians also preserved the memory of important events on buffalo hides. In the east, wampum belts were made of shell beads. The patterns and colors transmitted messages and recorded important events, such as treaties. In the nineteenth century, many imprisoned Indians made drawings in ledgers and on pieces of muslin cloth. These are now called Ledger Art.

The Europeans brought with them their tradition of books and binding. Printing was already well established in Europe and printing presses made their way to the New World. In 1539, the first printer came from Spain to Mexico where most of the books printed were religious texts in native languages for use by missionaries. Printing came to New England in 1638 eighteen years after the arrival of the Pilgrims in conjunction with the beginning of Harvard College.

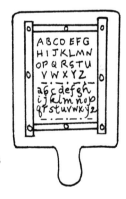

The important books in colonial times were the Bible, books of psalms and sermons, and yearly almanacs, which were considered necessities and hung by a string near the door. The most famous is *Poor Richard's Almanac* by Benjamin Franklin, who was then known as a printer. When he decided to write as well as print the almanac to save the author's fee, he used the pseudonym Richard Saunders. Students in colonial times learned from hornbooks, paddle-shaped pieces of wood with instructional papers protected by a layer of translucent horn from oxen.

As technology hastened the printing process and developed ways of making paper from wood pulp, books became more widespread. The book in America since the coming of the Europeans is distinguished more by the development of the content than by the form.

WINTER COUNT

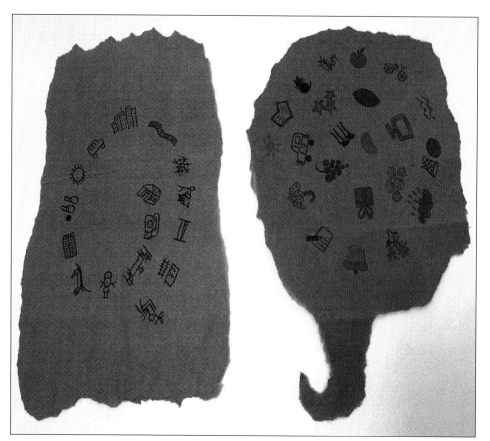

DAKOTA, NORTH AMERICA

Left: Brown grocery bag with black marker. / Right: Brown grocery bag with colored markers.

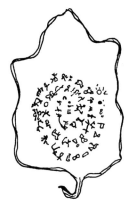

The Dakota Indians of the Great Plains recorded their history in Winter Counts made of buffalo skins. Each winter a picture was drawn on the buffalo skin to represent the significant event of the year. The Dakota did not call the years by numbers but gave them names instead. In the winter of 1883-84 there was a great meteor shower and the year was called "plenty-stars winter."

Make a *Winter Count* of your own life. It can represent each year with a picture, or go day by day or week by week. While the yearly count is traditional, a daily count over several weeks is easier to keep track of and do.

You'll Need:

- Front or back panel of grocery bag

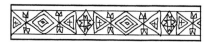 # Make the Book

Tear the grocery bag panel to make the "skin." You can keep it rectangular by tearing around the edges or shape it more like a "skin." You can make a pencil outline first or just tear directly.

 # Fill the Book

Draw pictures on the paper to represent years or days. The following pictures illustrate four days in winter.

1. We built a snowman. 2. We went sledding. 3. I went to the library. 4. It was a sunny day.

The illustrations usually started at the center and continued in a spiral. It is helpful to draw the spiral lightly in pencil first.

 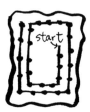

 ## Vary the Book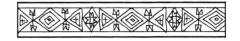

Give your winter count texture by crumpling and uncrumpling the grocery bag panel several times. You can enhance the color by rubbing it with the side of a brown crayon without its wrapper.

Use color. While the Dakota winter counts were primarily to record events, more decorative works on buffalo hides were made by many Native Americans living on the plains. Some were used as robes or tepee covers. Many skins told the story of one particular event or used symbolic drawings to represent an individual or family.

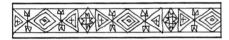 ## Read a Book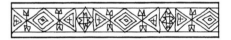

The Legend of the Indian Paintbrush, Tomie dePaola. New York: Putnam, 1988. The legend of how the flower, the Indian Paintbrush, got its name tells the story of a young boy who finds his calling as an artist painting on buffalo hides.

Storm Maker's Tipi, Paul Goble. New York: Atheneum Books for Young Readers, 2001. Sacred Hunter, a leader of the Blackfoot, was saved during a blizzard by Storm Maker, the Bad Weather Spirit, and given designs to paint on his tipi. There is information on tipi construction as well as a beautifully illustrated story.

Dancing Tepees: Poems of American Indian Youth, Virginia Driving Hawk Sneve, ed. New York: Holiday House, 1989. These poems are a collection of traditional ceremonial prayers and chants, lullabies and other tribal songs, and poems by contemporary tribal poets and include a Dakota Elk Song and an Osage Prayer Before Young Man's First Buffalo Hunt. They celebrate the spoken word tradition of Native Americans.

TIME LINE ACCORDION

MEXICO · CENTRAL AMERICA

Back: A record of four decades with events from family, politics, sports, fashion, music, books. Accordion from front panel of grocery bag, time line of braided yarn. / Front Left: History of paper. Accordion from one sheet of newspaper folded in half the long way and glued. Time line of videotape. / Front Right: Life cycle of a butterfly. Accordion from front panel of grocery bag cut in half the long way. Time line of found string.

Time was an important subject in Mayan and Aztec books which contained histories and calendars to keep track of what rituals needed to take place during the year. The books were made from folded deerskin or amatyl paper which was made from the inner bark of the fig tree. The pages were often coated with a lime wash for a smooth, white surface. Small pictures called glyphs formed the text. The drawing to the left is the glyph for the Aztec king Montezuma. There were also vibrant illustrations in rich colors.

This project is based on the Aztec and Mayan books in theme and basic form but adds a ribbon woven through the pages to act as a time line. Your time line can reflect historical events, your life or your family's life, or events in nature like the life cycle of a butterfly. Eight dates, two per page, will fit comfortably in the book. You can also have four separate events with an illustration for each.

Young children should be able to fold the accordion (I've done it with three-year-olds), but will probably need help with the hole punching.

You'll Need:

- 1 piece of long paper

- 1 piece of yarn or ribbon, twice the length of the paper plus a little extra or Long Measure x 2 (See page 9.) If you use ribbon, cut the ends on the diagonal.

- Hole punch

1. Fold a four page accordion:

a. Fold the paper in half. If it has writing on one side, it should be on the inside.

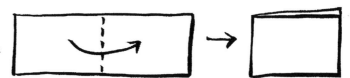

b. Fold the top layer in half by bringing the edge back to meet the fold.

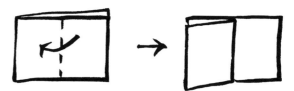

c. Turn the paper over so that the large side is on top.

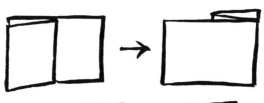

d. Bring the edge to meet the fold and crease.

2. Punch holes for threading:

a. On one side of the book, center the punch from top to bottom. Push it in as far as it will go. Punch a hole through all the layers.

b. Repeat on the other side.

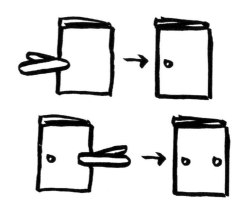

3. Thread the yarn, or ribbon, through the holes:

a. Set the book in front of you so that it looks like a "W" if you look at it from the side. From the outside, push the yarn through the top hole. It doesn't matter which side you start on.

b. Open the book gently and pull about a hand-length of yarn through.

c. Push the yarn through the next hole on the same page.

d. Flip the book over to the "M" side. Bring the yarn over the mountain and push the end through the next hole which is on the next page.

e. Flip the book over to the "W" side. Pull some more yarn through and push the end of the yarn through next hole on the same page.

f. Flip the book over to the "M" side. Push the end of the yarn through next hole which is on the next page.

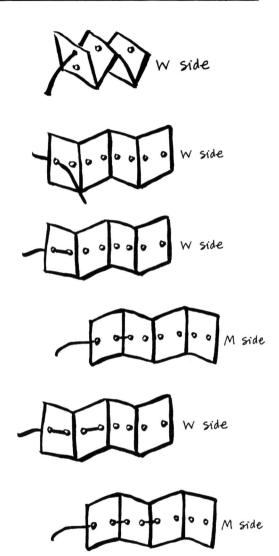

g. Flip the book over to the "W" side. Repeat the process until the yarn is threaded through all the holes. Be careful not to miss any. The "W" side will have four long lines of yarn and the "M" side will have three short lines.

h. Gently pull the yarn through so that there is an even amount extending beyond the edges on both sides.

To close the book: Stand the book to make a "W" again. Put the end of the yarn coming from the one side of the book over the top of the open "W" to the other side. Put the other end of the yarn over the top of the open "W" in the opposite direction. Wrap the yarn around the book and tie a bow at the bottom of the "W."

 ## Vary the Book

Make longer time lines. For books with more pages, follow the directions for making a *Curandero Book* on page 63.

Use a front or back grocery panel to make a taller time line. Each page can represent a decade or a year and record historical, cultural and personal events. This is a fun project for a family, class or group of friends.

Make a book with a red ribbon for Valentine's Day. I first made this style of book as a valentine. When I showed it to my son's preschool teacher, she said, "Hand-eye coordination." We made dinosaur time lines.

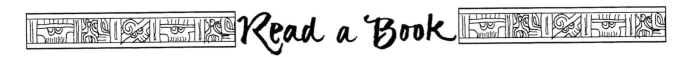

Read a Book

The Flame of Peace: A Tale of the Aztecs, Deborah Nourse Lattimore. New York: HarperTrophy, 1987. A young Aztec boy, Two Flint, braves nine evil demons and brings the magic flame of peace to his people. The illustrations by the author are inspired by Aztec manuscripts. The page numbers are written in Aztec as well as Arabic numerals.

Rain Player, David Wisniewski. New York: Clarion Books, 1991. A Mayan boy must defeat Chac, the god of rain, in a ball game. If he loses, he will turn into a frog. If he wins, he will end the drought. The author has illustrated the book with dramatic cut-paper illustrations. The story begins with a picture of an old priest holding an accordion book.

COMIC BOOK

UNITED STATES OF AMERICA

Back: Book (closed and open) made from Sunday newspaper comic page with the blank margins trimmed. Writing and illustrations done on used copy paper and glued in. / Front: Book from one sheet of used copy paper. Writing done with black marker. Illustration: black marker and colored pencils.

Handmade Books for a Healthy Planet/ ©2010 Susan Kapuscinski Gaylord /makingbooks.com

In the twentieth century, the United States became known for the popular culture it exported throughout the world. The comic book can be considered the book form of popular culture. While there were many precursors, the comic book as we know it began in the 1930s at Eastern Color Printing in New York which printed the color funnies in Sunday newspapers. Since the color presses weren't used all the time, Sales Manager Harry Wildenberg folded a color printed newspaper sheet into a booklet and created the comic book. The first comic books were reprints of comic strips. Their success led to new characters and stories, created just for the comic books.

Comic books cover a wide range of stories from superheroes to Archie. You can create your own characters, use myths from different cultures as a source, or write about local heroes who make the community a better place.

You'll Need:

- 1 piece of paper
- Scissors

1. Fold the paper in half so that it is long and skinny like a hot dog. If it has writing on one side, the writing should be on the inside.

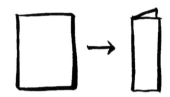

2. Open the paper and fold it in half the other way so that it is like a hamburger.

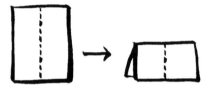

3. Take one layer of paper, flip the edge back to meet the fold, and crease.

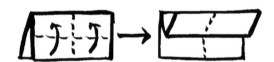

4. Turn the paper over, flip the edge of the paper back up to meet the fold, and crease.

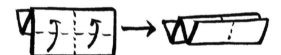

5. Place the paper on the table so that you see a "W" when you look at the end.

6. Hold the center of the "W" and cut along the center fold. You'll be cutting through two layers of paper and stopping at the cross fold.

fold at center of "W"

7. With your wrists above your fingers, hold the "W" on either side of the center cut. Turn your wrists to the sides. You will have an open book with four sections.

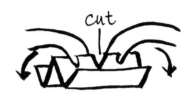

cut

8. Gather the sections together in your hand and press together to make a flat book. Smooth along the fold.

 # Vary the Book

Make the book from the comics page of the newspaper. Cut away the white margins on the sides of the page for a more lively background. Write and illustrate your comics on separate pieces of paper and glue the pages into the book.

Publish the comic books. Use US Letter/A4 paper. Make a book and do the writing and drawing with black pen or marker. Open the book so that it is a flat sheet of paper again. All the writing and drawing is on the same side. Place the paper on a copier or scanner. Print, fold and cut as many copies as you want.

 # Read a Book

Wingman, Daniel Pinkwater. New York: Dodd, Mead, 1975. Chinese-American Donald Chen escapes from his troubles at school by reading comics under the George Washington Bridge. Wingman, a comic hero come to life, and a new teacher help Donald discover new abilities and make friends.

Little Lit: It Was a Dark and Silly Night, Art Spiegelman and Françoise Mouly, ed. New York: RAW Junior LLC, 2003. Art Speigelman, who brought the graphic novel for adults to prominence with *Maus*, has gathered work from well-known authors and artists including Lemony Snicket and Neil Gaiman. Also in the series is *Little Lit: Once Upon a Time*.

Greek Myths for Young Children, Marcia Williams. Cambridge, Massachusetts: Candlewick Press, 1995. Marcia Williams presents eight Greek myths in comic book format with a wonderful combination of simple storytelling, humor, and wit. She has written and illustrated many other books in a similar format, including *The Iliad and The Odyssey, Tales from William Shakespeare*, and *King Arthur and the Knights of the Round Table*.

CURANDERO BOOK

MEXICO

Back Left: Closed book: Cereal box covered with newspaper. Title and illustrations cut from grocery bag. / Back Right: Four page accordion from grocery bag. Cereal box cover covered with newspaper. Illustrations cut from newspaper. / Front: Accordion from two sheets of US Letter/A4 used copy paper. Illustrations cut from grocery bags.

The healers of the Otomi Indians in the village of San Pablito, Mexico use bark paper cutouts of figures in ceremonies to bring rain for the crops, heal the sick and keep away evil spirits. They also make curandero books which describe the figures that are used. To make the amate paper, the Otomi boil strips of the inner bark of the fig tree to soften them, then lay them out in a grid on a flat stone and pound them with a board until the fibers mesh together. The paper is used for the pages and the covers of the books as well as for the figures.

I called my *Curandero Book* a *Book to Heal The Spirit* and wrote about what makes me feel better when I am sad. Cut your illustrations from brown grocery bags to look like bark paper or use other papers, such as newspaper or catalog pages, for color.

For younger children or quicker projects, make a four page accordion, with or without a cover. Draw pictures instead of cutting and gluing.

You'll Need:

- 2 pieces of long paper
- 1 cereal box panel
- Paper to cover the covers
- Paper for illustrations
- Glue stick and scrap paper
- Scissors

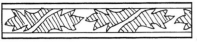 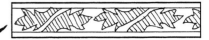
1. Fold two 4-page accordion sections:

a. Put both pieces of paper together and tap to make them even. If the paper has writing on one side, the writing should be showing. Holding the two pieces together, fold a tab at one end about a thumb-width wide.

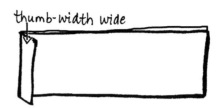

b. Separate the pieces of paper.

c. One at a time, fold each piece of paper in half with the tab on the inside. The writing should be on the inside,

d. Fold the top half in half by bringing the edge back to meet the fold.

e. Turn the paper over so that the large side is on top.

f. Bring the edge to meet the fold and crease.

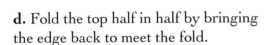

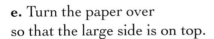

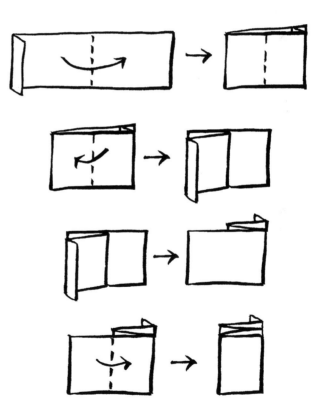

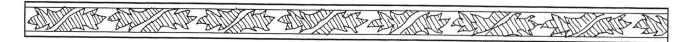

2. Attach the sections together:

a. Place the two folded sections in front of you so that the tabs are on the top and they look like envelopes.

b. Place a piece of scrap paper under one of the tabs. Cover the entire tab with a thin coat of glue. Remove the scrap paper and fold it in half with the glue on the inside so nothing will stick to it.

c. Place the back of the section without the glue on top of the tab with the glue. You'll notice there is a tab showing on the top. Open the accordion and press along the glued tab to help the glue adhere.

d. Trim off the tab.

3. Attach the book and cut front cover:

a. Open the front page of the accordion. Insert a piece of scrap paper and close.

b. Cover the entire surface with a thin coat of glue. Keeping the pages folded, remove the scrap paper and fold it in half with the glue on the inside so nothing will stick to it.

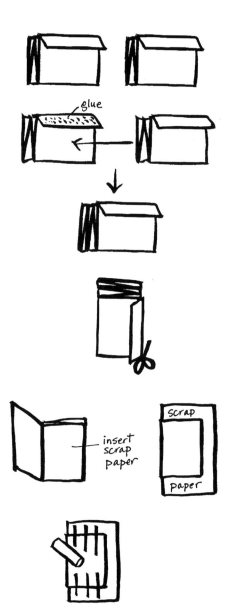

c. Place the cereal box panel so that it is wider than it is tall.

d. Leaving a very small border of cereal box, place the glued side of the folded pages on the neatest corner of the cereal box panel. Press firmly. Open the pages, smooth with your hand to help the glue adhere, and close.

e. Leaving a matching small border on the other two sides, draw lines and then cut out the cover.

4. Cut the back cover:

Line up 2 sides of the book in the neatest corner of the cereal box panel. Trace around the other two sides and cut out. You now have a back cover.

5. Attach the back cover:

a. Open the back page and insert scrap paper. Cover the entire surface with a thin coat of glue. Keeping the pages folded, remove the scrap paper and fold it in half with the glue on the inside so nothing will stick to it.

b. Making sure the front and back covers are lined up evenly, place the back cover on the book. Press firmly. Open the pages and smooth with your hand to help the glue adhere.

6. Cover the covers:

a. Place the book on the cover paper and trace around the book. Repeat for the second cover. Cut out.

b. Place a piece of cover paper with the side you want to show face down on a piece of scrap paper. Cover the entire surface with glue.

c. Place the cover paper on the front cover and smooth to help the glue adhere. Repeat on the back cover.

Fill the Book

Make a book describing what heals your spirit and makes you feel better when you are sad. Most of the traditional papercuts from San Pablito are symmetrical. If you wish to make yours symmetrical, fold the paper in half with the side you want showing on the inside. Draw half the design and then cut. When you glue the illustrations into the book, remember to cover the whole surface of the back side of your image with glue and use scrap paper.

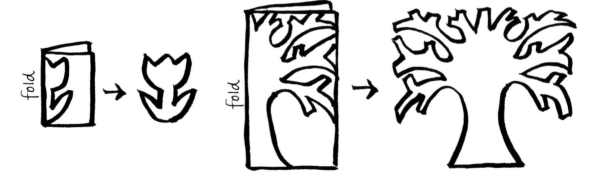

Handmade Books for a Healthy Planet/ ©2010 Susan Kapuscinski Gaylord /makingbooks.com

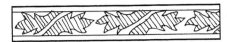 # Vary the Book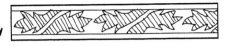

Add yarn or ribbon before attaching the back cover by following the directions in *Seasons Accordion Book* on page 85.

Think about what things in the world need healing—sick and hungry children, areas of the world in war and conflict, the environment—and make healing books for them. Make your own book or work with others. More pages can be added by folding additional four page accordions with tabs and attaching them. The last tab is cut off.

 # Read a Book

Cuckoo: A Mexican Folktale, Lois Ehlert. New York: Harcourt Brace & Company, 1997. The bilingual *Cuckoo* tells the story of the cuckoo, a pretty bird with a pretty song who was vain and too lazy to help the other birds collect seeds. When a fire started in the field, it was cuckoo who saved the seeds. Her beautiful song turned to a raspy "cuckoo" and her beautiful feathers were scorched. Illustrated with vibrant cutouts inspired by Mexican crafts and folk art, this book can be an inspiration for your illustrations.

The Corn Grows Ripe, Dorothy Rhoads, illustrated by Jean Charlot. New York: Puffin Books, 1956. In this short chapter book, a Mayan village comes to life through the story of a young boy who is known as Tigre. An injury to his father causes the lighthearted and a little bit lazy Tigre to take responsibility for clearing, burning and planting the cornfield.

The Mouse Bride: A Mayan Folk Tale, Judith Dupre, illustrated by Fabricio Vanden Broeck. New York: Alfred A. Knopf, 1993. This is a beautifully illustrated telling of a folktale that is told in various versions around the world. Two mice seek the most powerful being in the universe to marry their daughter. They are sent from the Sun to the Cloud to the Wind to the Wall who tells them that the mouse is the most powerful of all because he can make the Wall crumble from his burrowing.

Asia

 The history of the book began in western Asia. The earliest books were tablets of clay from Mesopotamia that were first made in about 4,000 BCE. The writing, called cuneiform, was a series of wedge-shaped marks made on soft clay tablets with a reed stylus. The soft clay was hardened in the sun to make durable books. There were legal documents and texts on astronomy, medicine, poetry and religious matters. They were stored in libraries and carefully indexed.

Two other traditions in western Asia use animal skin as their primary material: the scrolls of the Hebrews and the books of Persia and Arabia that use the Western codex style of binding with folded sheets sewn along the fold. The Hebrew scrolls, made first of leather and later vellum, were mounted on two rods. The form is still used today for writing the Torah. The books of Persia and Arabia, which include the Koran as well as secular titles, were written first on vellum or parchment and later on paper.

Of the books of eastern Asia, the richest tradition, in terms of variety of form, is that of China. The development of books in China, from the scroll onward, spread to Japan and Korea.

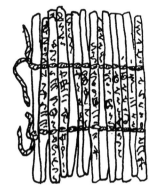 The first books, *jian ce*, or slat books, were made of strips of wood or bamboo bound together by cord. They date from about 1,700 BCE and were in use until the fourth century CE. The writing was done with a brush and ink. Books made with narrow slats were rolled up when not in use. Wider slats were folded accordion style. It is believed that Chinese is written vertically because of the shape of these early books.

The slat books gave way to scrolls made of silk. Although silk was more expensive, the scroll was more convenient to carry and to store. The end of the scroll was attached to a wooden roller. Special scrolls sometimes had rollers made of jade. A blank piece of silk was attached to the end to act as a cover, protecting the rolled scroll. Silk was gradually replaced by the less expensive paper, the invention of which is attributed to Cai Lun in 105 CE.

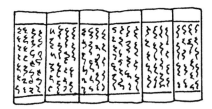

In another shift toward convenience, the scroll evolved into the accordion book when the paper was folded rather than rolled. Accordion books could be stored flat and were easier to use. Trying to find a particular passage in the middle of a scroll involved a lot of rolling and unrolling. The accordion book came into prominent use in the mid-ninth century, primarily for writing the Buddhist scriptures which are called *sutras*. Its Chinese name, *ching-che-chuang*, means "sutra binding."

The next step in the evolution of books in China was a book of folded and sewn leaves. Several transitional styles led the way to the stitched binding of the Ming Dynasty in the sixteenth century. These books were made by folding sheets of paper in half, stacking the sheets individually, and sewing them together at the open edge. The books were all soft cover. Each chapter of a book would be bound separately with the entire set of volumes comprising the book. They were often stored between boards or in cases and laid flat on bookshelves. This style was common until the mid-twentieth century when it began to be replaced by Western bindings.

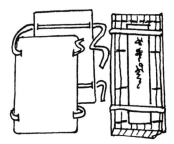

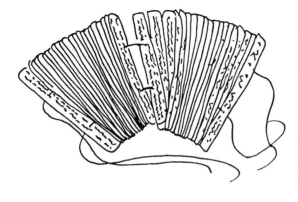

The other main center of book development in eastern Asia was India. The primary form, made of palm leaves strung together, was in common use by the end of the fourth century. The long leaves of the palm tree were cut into rectangular shapes, boiled in water or milk, dried, and rubbed with a shell or stone to make them smooth. The writing was incised into the leaves with a metal stylus. To make the writing visible, ink was rubbed over the leaf where it went into the incised lines. The excess ink was then wiped off. The reason for the rounded character of Indian scripts is because straight horizontal strokes would have split the leaves. The leaves have one, two, or three holes and are strung on cords. Coins, rings or beads tied to the ends of the cords keep the book together. Some books have decorated wooden covers.

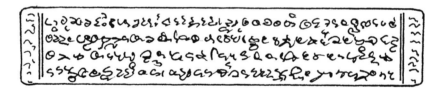

The palm leaf form spread to Indonesia and Southeast Asia. Even when different materials were used, such as bamboo in Indonesia and lacquered cloth, ivory and metal in Southeast Asia, the long rectangular shape remained. Books of a similar shape were also made in Tibet and Bhutan. There, unattached paper pages were stacked between wooden covers that were then wrapped in cloth. The accordion form was also used in India and Southeast Asia.

PALM LEAF BOOK

INDIA · INDONESIA · SOUTHEAST ASIA

Back Left: Book pages made from two pieces of recycled paper glued together, with yarn and pony beads. Back Right: Book pages made from a granola bar box, with curling ribbon, saved from a gift, and buttons. Front: Book pages made from discarded CDs, with strips cut from a plastic rice cake bag, milk container tops, and bread closures.

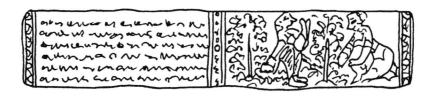

Rectangular books of palm leaves are the traditional form of India, Indonesia, and Southeast Asia. The leaves have one, two, or three holes and are strung together on a cord. Knots, rings, beads or coins at each end of the cord keep the book together.

The book contains four pages—a title page followed by three pages with a text that creates a sequence. The page design is inspired by a page from an Oriya manuscript from India, a drawing of which is pictured above. A center border divides the pages, one side for the text and one side for the illustrations. I keep it simple with one hole so that there are only two knots to tie.

For young children, cut the strips ahead. It will be easier for them to punch the holes if you use two sheets of paper glued together rather than a cereal box panel. I suggest treating the ends of the yarn to make it easier to thread. (See page 17.) Be prepared to help with the knots.

You'll Need:

- 1 cereal box panel or 2 pieces of used paper glued together with the writing sides facing each other

- 1 piece of yarn or curling ribbon, the length of the cereal box or Short Measure x 1 (See page 9.)

- 2 pony beads, plastic bread closures, or buttons

- Scissors

- Hole Punch

- Pencil

1. Punch holes and cut the pages:

a. Place the cereal box panel in front of you so that it is taller than wide. At the center of the bottom edge, push the hole punch in as far as it will go and punch a hole.

push punch in as far as it will go

b. Make one palm leaf page by cutting above the hole so that the hole is in the center of the page from top to bottom. You may find it easier to draw the line in pencil before you cut. If the line and your cutting isn't exactly straight, don't worry about it.

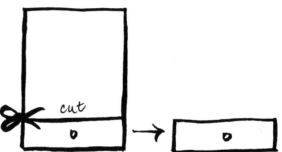

cut

c. Make three more pages. Repeat the same process of punching a hole and cutting above or use the page you have made as a guide and cut the page first and then punch the hole.

2. Tie the bead to one end of the yarn:

a. Put the yarn through the hole in the bead. The bead should be about a thumb-length from one end of the yarn.

b. Tie a knot around the bead so that the bead is inside the knot.

c. Tighten the knot around the bead.

d. Tie a second knot to secure it. Tug on the bead to tighten the knot.

bead thumb-length from end

3. String the pages on the yarn and tie on the second bead:

a. Starting with the end of the yarn without a bead, push the yarn through the holes in the pages.

b. Put the other end of the yarn through the hole in the bead about a thumb-length from the end. Tie the bead onto the yarn.

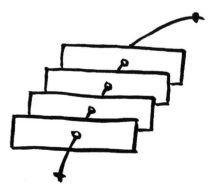

On each page, draw a border on either side of the center hole. Draw a border on each end of the page. Write the text on the left side and draw an illustration on the right side.

Read the book by flipping the pages forward. Because there is only one center hole, the pages can spin around. Don't worry if a page is upside down as you read the book. Just turn it around to get it right-side-up.

To close the book: Pull the yarn so that the front bead is resting against the front of the book. Wrap the yarn around the book and tuck the back bead under the yarn.

 # Vary the Book

Make wider books with three holes. Place the cereal box panel in front of you so that it is wider than tall. Punch the center holes and cut pages. For the two side holes, push the punch in as far as it will go at each side edge and punch. For a book with two holes, leave out the center hole and just punch a hole on each side.

Make a book about the planets with one page for each planet. Draw a picture and put facts—the size, the number of moons, and the distance from the sun.

Use for book reports. Use separate pages for beginning, middle and end. Make longer books with more pages for significant events in the plot or character descriptions.

Read a Book

Rama and Sita: A Tale from Ancient Java, David Weitzman. Boston: David R. Godine, Publisher, 2002. Taken from the Hindu epic *The Ramayana* or *Rama's Way*, Rama and Sita is full of adventure, intrigue, loyalty and devotion. The striking illustrations are modeled after Javanese shadow puppets. I have two palm leaf books from Bali which tell the story of *The Ramayana*.

How Ganesh Got His Elephant Head, Harish Johari and Vatsala Sperling, illustrated by Pieter Weltevrede. Rochester, Vermont: Bear Club Books, 2003. The story of how Ganesh, well loved as the god who has the power to make good things happen, got his elephant head is illustrated with paintings using traditional Indian techniques.

Silent Lotus, Jeanne M. Lee. New York: Farrar, Straus and Giroux, 1991. This beautifully illustrated story, set in long ago Cambodia, tells of a young girl who cannot hear or speak and becomes the most famous dancer in the Khmer court.

MATH SLAT BOOK

ANCIENT CHINA

Back: Counting book of family trip to Percé, Québec. Slats made from cereal boxes covered with the map we used on the trip. Numbers and pictures done on recycled paper and glued on. Front Left: Multiplication facts book. Slats made from cleaned popsicle sticks. Writing done with marker. Front Right: Multiplication book with a couplet rhyme for each fact and arrays of dots made with marker on the left side. Slats from cereal boxes.

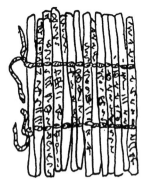

One of the primary functions of early books in many cultures was for mathematics. Books were used to keep records of property owned and traded, business transactions, and tributes offered to kings and emperors. I was inspired by a picture of China's earliest book form, the slat book. The inventory of weapons from 93 to 95 CE during the Han Dynasty contained seventy-seven wooden strips, each nine inches high and one-half inch wide.

Your *Slat Book* can be held vertically for a counting book or horizontally for a study guide for math facts. The counting book can have numbers on the top, pictures and descriptions in the center, and words on the bottom. It can be about anything that interests you: animals, trees, a trip, a country, your house. While the idea of how to put this book together is simple, the assembly can be tricky because the knots must be tied tightly against the slats to keep the book together. In a group, I find it best to work in pairs, with one person holding the slats while the other ties.

If you make the book with young children, they can hold the slats while an adult ties the yarn.

You'll Need:

- 2 cereal box panels (3 if small) and
- 2 pieces of yarn, 2 arm-lengths or Short Measure x 4 (See page 9.)

  or

- 10 cleaned popsicle sticks and
- 2 pieces of yarn, 5 times length of sticks or Short Measure x 4 (See page 9.)

- Scissors

- Pencil

- White Glue

1. Cut slats if using cereal box panels:

Place the cereal box panel in front of you so that it is taller than wide. Make a pencil mark one thumb-length from the bottom. Use the mark as a guide to cut one slat from the panel. You may find it easier to draw the line in pencil before you cut. If the line and your cutting aren't exactly straight, don't worry about it. Using the slat you have just made as a guide, cut 9 more slats.

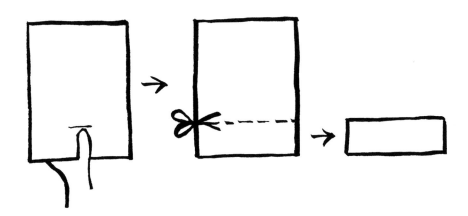

2. Tie slats together:

a. Fold each piece of yarn in half.

b. Insert a slat into the fold of one piece of yarn so that the yarn is about one thumb-end from the one end of the slat. Tie a single knot, making sure that the knot is at the bottom of the slat. Pull on the yarn so that the knot is tight against the slat. The yarn should grip enough to stay in place while you tie a second knot to make a double knot.

c. Tie the second piece of yarn around the slat, about one thumb-end from the other end of the slat.

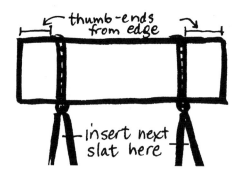

d. Insert the next slat between the pieces of yarn and tie double knots. It will be easier if the slat you are tying is close to the edge of the table or desk. Because the slat tends to move while you are tying the knot, you may want to have a partner hold the slat or place something on top to keep it from moving.

e. Repeat until all the slats are tied together.

Since the yarn stretches with time, I like to anchor it with glue. Squeeze white glue under the yarn and press lightly on the yarn to make sure it adheres. It will dry clear so don't worry if it seeps out from under the yarn. Let it dry flat before you move it.

To close the book: Either fold the slats like an accordion or roll the slats like a scroll. Any extra yarn can be wrapped around the book.

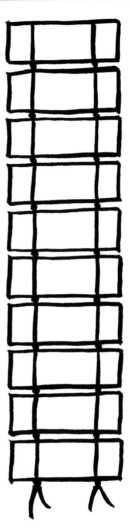

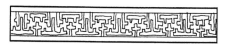 Vary the Book

Make name books with one letter per slat. Write a name acrostic with one line per slat. Jen: J is for joy. E is for excellence. N is for noble.

Make a multiplication fact book with cereal box slats. Combine the Chinese book tradition with the 19th century American way of teaching the facts with couplet rhymes: *4 x 7 are 28, I push open the garden gate.*

Collaborate on a group book. Each person writes his name on a slat and decorates it to reflect his personality and interests. Write names horizontally for a book that can hang on the wall, vertically for a book that can stand like an accordion on a table. This is an excellent introduction project for a class or group or a fun family activity. Don't forget to include your pets.

 Read a Book

A Grain of Rice, Helena Clare Pittman. New York: Hastings House Publishers, 1986. Set in fifteenth-century China, this is the story of a humble peasant who wins the hand of a princess in marriage by using math.

The Warlord's Beads, Virginia Walton Pilegard, illustrated by Nicolas Debon. Gretna, LA: Pelican Publishing Company, Inc., 2001. Chuan's father's job is to count the Warlord's treasures. When he has so many to count that he loses track, Chuan saves his father by inventing a counting frame using beads and the switches the Warlord's sons use to torment him. The counting frame was the forerunner of the abacus.

Count Your Way Through China, Jim Haskins. Minneapolis: Carolrhoda Books, Inc., 1987. Information about China is presented through the numbers one to ten. One slightly jarring note is the illustration of "eight volumes" in which the books have Western bindings.

SEASONS ACCORDION BOOK

CHINA

Left: Closed book. Cereal box cover decorated with collage box pieces. Yarn tie. / Center: Accordion from recycled folded US Letter/A4 paper. Cover from cereal box. Illustrations cut from gift wrap scraps and can and tea labels. Right: Accordion from grocery bag. Text and illustration done on used copy paper and glued in.

Accordion books with hard covers were first made in China and then spread to Japan and Korea. Traditionally the books contained sutras (Buddhist scriptures) or were albums of calligraphy or painting. The Seasons Accordion Book was inspired by an accordion book I purchased in Chinatown in Boston. Written in Chinese and English, it is called Long Established Customs at Chinese Festivals. Since many of the festivals are related to the seasons, they were chosen as the theme of the book.

There are four pages, one for each season. The writing can be about natural occurrences (weather and growth cycles), holidays celebrated, or seasonal activities (swimming and sledding). The illustrations can be small detailed pictures, simple drawings or cut paper collages that function as emblems for the seasons.

You can use yarn or ribbon for the tie. Ribbon will lie flatter. Yarn will leave a bump in the back page.

You'll Need:

- 1 piece of long paper
- 1 cereal box panel
- 1 piece of yarn or ribbon, twice the length of the paper or Short Measure x 2 (See page 9.)
- Glue stick and scrap paper
- Scissors
- Pencil

1. Fold a four page accordion:

a. Fold the paper in half.

b. Fold the top layer in half by bringing the edge back to meet the fold.

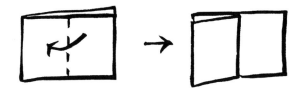

c. Turn the paper over so that the large side is on top.

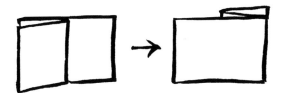

d. Bring the edge to meet the fold and crease.

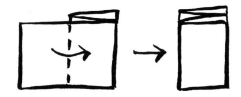

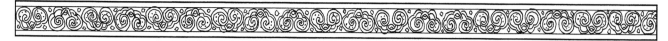

2. Attach and cut the front cover:

a. Open the front page of the accordion. Insert a piece of scrap paper and close.

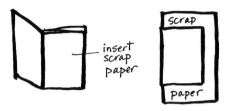

b. Cover the entire surface with a thin coat of glue. Keeping the pages folded, remove the scrap paper and fold it in half with the glue on the inside so nothing will stick to it.

c. Decide whether you want the cover to show the outside or the inside of the cereal box panel. Place the box panel in front of you so that is wider than it is tall with the side you do not want for the cover on the top.

d. Leaving a very small border, place the glued side of the folded pages on the neatest corner of the cereal box panel. Press firmly. Open the pages, smooth with your hand to help the glue adhere, and close.

e. Leaving a matching small border on the other two sides, draw lines and cut the cover.

3. Cut the back cover:

Line up 2 sides of the book in the neatest corner of the cereal box panel. Trace around the other two sides and cut out. You now have a back cover.

4. Attach the tie and back cover:

a. Open the back page and insert scrap paper. Cover the entire surface with a thin coat of glue. Keeping the pages folded, remove the scrap paper and fold it in half with the glue on the inside so nothing will stick to it.

b. Place the yarn or ribbon across the center of the back page with the center of the yarn in the center of the page. A good way to center the yarn is to hold the book up and adjust the ends so they are even.

glue

adjust ends so they are even

c. Making sure the front and back covers are lined up evenly, place the back cover on the book. Press firmly. Open the pages and smooth down to help the glue adhere.

To write the text and draw the illustrations on the pages:
a. Place the book on the table with the back cover (the one with the tie) on the bottom. Open the book to the left.

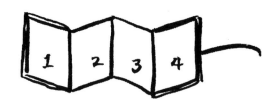

b. Write the text and draw the illustrations on the pages. Page 1 is on the left.

To close the book: Fold it up and tie it in front with a bow.

 # Vary the Book

Pick a tree and record its changes, using one page for each season.

The books can contain additional pages. The *Curandero Book* on page 63 has directions for longer accordion books. A *Seasons Book* with eight pages would give room to alternate text and illustrations on separate pages.

A twelve-page book may be used for Chinese New Year, with one page for each sign of the zodiac. Since red is the traditional color of celebrations and the new year, red covers would be especially appropriate.

Lao Lao of Dragon Mountain, Margaret Bateson-Hill, illustrated by Francesca Pelizzoli. London: DeAgnosti Editions, 1996. An old woman named Lao Lao, who entertained her village by making beautiful and delicate paper cuts, was saved from the jealous emperor by the Ice Dragon. She now rides on the dragon's back covering the trees with blossoms in spring, filling the fields with flowers in summer, providing apples and nuts in autumn, and scattering snowflakes in winter. The beautifully designed and illustrated book includes instructions on how to make a snowflake, a butterfly, a flower, and a dragon from cut paper which you could use to illustrate your *Seasons Book.*

Dragon Kite of the Autumn Moon, Valerie Reddix. New York: Lothrop, Lee and Shephard, 1991. Kite day is celebrated in Taiwan on the ninth day of the ninth month. Kites, which are flown during the day, are set free at night to carry one's misfortunes away and burned on their return to earth. In this touching story, the young Tad-tin sacrifices his beloved dragon kite to help his ailing grandfather.

Cat and Rat: The Legend of the Chinese Zodiac, Ed Young. New York: Henry Holt and Company, 1995. The emperor holds a race to choose the twelve animals of the zodiac. Through cleverness, Rat is the first animal to cross the finish line. Cat loses the twelfth spot to Pig.

Mouse Match: A Chinese Folktale, Ed Young. New York: Harcourt, 1997. The Chinese version of a folktale that is told in various ways around the world. Two mice seek the most powerful being in the universe to marry their daughter. They are sent from the Sun to the Cloud to the Wind to the Wall who tells them that the mouse is the most powerful of all because he can make the Wall crumble from his burrowing. This book is in the accordion book format.

BOOK OF HAIKU

JAPAN

Left: Haiku by Basho. Illustrations from collage box papers and adhesive-backed pieces saved from stamps. Center: Book made from half sheets of recycled US Letter/A4 paper. Cover from cereal box. Binding with curling ribbon from gift packages. Right: Closed book. Stitching started in front with yard sale beads attached to the ends of the thread.

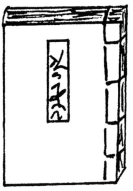

The Book of Haiku binds pages of Japanese haiku or other short poetry in the Asian tradition. A stack of individually folded pages are sewn together opposite the fold along the open ends, forming a pouch. Its Japanese name is fukuro toji, or pouch binding. This method of binding developed because very thin paper was used, and writing could be done on only one side of the paper. In the drawing, the binding is on the right side. That's because Japanese is read from right to left. You'll make your book with the binding on the left since we read from left to right.

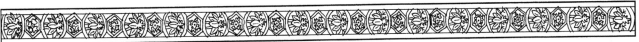

Write your own haiku or other short poems or collect haiku by Japanese masters of the form. See pages 99–100 for information on writing haiku. Illustrate your haiku with cut paper collage. Information on collage can be found on page 101.

Don't be intimidated by the length of directions. The binding is not difficult. There are lots of steps but they are not hard. There is something very satisfying about the extra weight of the pages that comes from the doubled sheet of paper. The book is a pleasure to write and create collages in, and to turn the pages as you read.

You'll Need:

- 7–9 pieces of used paper with writing on one side only (Two will be for the covers and may be a different color.)

- Crochet cotton or heavy thread, 4 times the height of the page or Long Measure x 2 for US Letter/A4 (See page 9.)

- Tapestry needle, size 16 preferred

- Pencil

- 2 Clothespins

- Nail

- 2 blocks of wood (one hand-length piece of two by four) or hammer and one block of wood

- Collage paper for illustrations

- Glue stick and scrap paper

- Scissors

1. One at a time, fold each piece of paper in half with the writing on the inside.

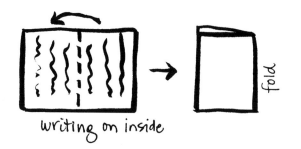

writing on inside

2. Make a vertical crease on the front cover which will be a guide for marking where the holes will go:

   a. Place the front cover so that the fold is on the right.

   b. At the center of the open (left) side, make a pencil mark a thumb-width from the edge.

pencil mark thumb-width from edge

fold

   c. At the pencil mark, fold back the top layer to make a narrow tab.

   d. Unfold the tab. Both layers will again be the same size. There will be a long crease which will be the guide line for marking where the holes will go.

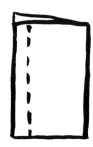

3. Make marks where the holes will go:

Make 5 small dots on the fold. Start by making a dot one thumb-end from the bottom and another one thumb-end from the top. Make a dot centered from top to bottom (just do it by eye). Make two more dots: one centered between the top dot and the center and the other centered between the center and the bottom dot, again by eye.

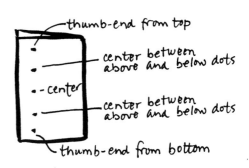

4. Make the holes:

a. Stack the folded papers with the folds on the right side: front cover on top, pages, back cover on bottom. Hold the entire stack in both hands with the folds at the bottom and tap it against the table to even the pages. Clip the stack together with two clothespins, one on the top edge and one on the bottom edge, about thumb-length from the open edges of the book. You'll leave the clothespins in place until the sewing is finished.

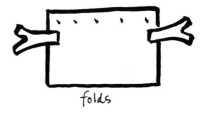

folds

b. Place one piece of wood on the table. Place the clipped book on top.

c. Place the nail on one of the dots. Hit the nail with the second block of wood three times and then check the holes. If you hammer too hard, you can nail the book to the wood. The holes do need to be fairly large. If you hold the book up to the light, you should be able to see a small circle of light. Continue until you have 5 holes.

5. Thread the needle:

If the needle has a large eye, tie the thread onto the needle with a double knot to keep it from slipping off. Do not tie a knot at the end. The thread will be used singly.

6. Sew the book:

There are two kinds of stitches. I call them wrapping stitches and long stitches. Wrapping stitches go around the edges of the book with the thread going in and out of the same hole. Long stitches stay on one side of the book and go from one hole to another. As you sew, check periodically to make sure the thread is taut but not digging into the edges.

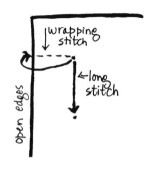

Here is an overview: You start at the top of the book from the back. You work down the book doing wrapping and long stitches. At each hole, you wrap the edge (or edges when you are at the top and bottom). You then move down to the next hole with a long stitch. As you work your way down the book, there will be some gaps in the long stitches. Don't worry about them, they will be filled in later. When you have wrapped all the edges including the bottom, it's time to work your way back up the book with long stitches and then tie the two ends together in a knot.

a. Start at the back of the book. Go into the top hole. Pull the thread through the hole until about an index finger-length of thread is left. Place the thread under the clothespin to hold it in place while you sew.

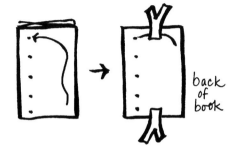

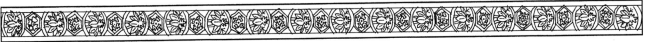

b. Wrapping stitch: Wrap the thread around the top of the book and go into Hole 1 from the back.

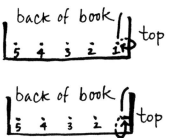

c. Wrapping stitch: Wrap the thread around the side of the book and go into Hole 1 from the back.

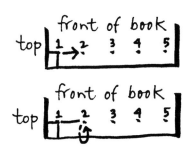

d. Long stitch: Turn the book over to the front. Make a long stitch down to Hole 2.

e. Wrapping stitch: Wrap the thread around the side of the book and go into Hole 2 from the front.

f. Long stitch: Turn the book over to the back. Make a long stitch down to Hole 3.

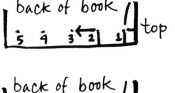

g. Wrapping stitch: Wrap the thread around the side of the book and go into Hole 3 from the back. You'll notice that there is an unfilled space. Don't worry. It will be filled later. When working with a group, I always go this far working step by step. From here, I let those who have the idea continue to *Step l* on their own.

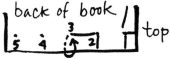

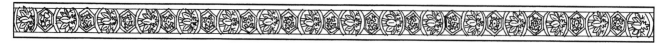

h. Long stitch: Turn the book over to the front. Make a long stitch down to Hole 4.

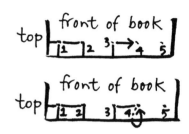

i. Wrapping stitch: Wrap the thread around the side of the book and go into Hole 4 from the front.

j. Long stitch: Turn the book over to the back. Make a long stitch down to Hole 5.

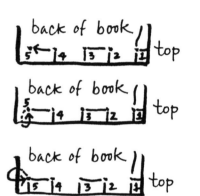

k. Wrapping stitch: Wrap the thread around the side of the book and go into Hole 5 from the back.

l. Wrapping stitch: Wrap the thread around the bottom edge of the book, and go into Hole 5 from the back. You have now wrapped all the edges and sides of the book.

m. Long stitch: Turn the book over to the front and go from Hole 5 to Hole 4.

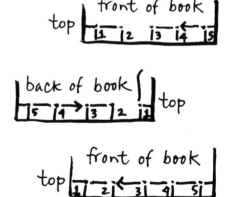

n. Long stitch: Turn the book over to the back and go from Hole 4 to Hole 3.

o. Long stitch: Turn the book over to the front and go from Hole 3 to Hole 2.

p. Turn the book over to the back. It is time to tie the two ends of the thread together. To make it easier to tie a knot, slip the needle under the top stitch to anchor the thread.

slip needle under top wrapped stitch

q. Unclip the book and take the needle off the thread. Tie the two ends in a double knot with the knot over Hole 1. If you know how to tie a square knot, do so.

back of book — tie double knot

r. If the ends of the thread are long, trim them so that they are about a thumb-end long. Do not cut any closer to the knot. If you clip the ends too close to the knot, it may unravel.

Fill the Book

1. Write or collect five to seven haiku.

The information on writing haiku comes from two sources: *The Haiku Handbook: How to Write, Share, and Teach Haiku* by William J. Higginson (McGraw Hill, 1985) and a conversation with Lowell, Massachusetts poet Paul Marion whose poems are quoted here. While many of us learned haiku as three line, seventeen syllable poems, it is not necessary to observe these restrictions. The idea of haiku is to say a lot with a little. It is about writing images, or word pictures, and writing them briefly. Connecting and descriptive words are left out. There are no similes, metaphors, or other literary devices. The haiku shown here are all three lines. The three line form is used frequently and is a good starting point, but the poems can be shorter or longer.

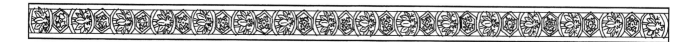

While I don't consider myself particularly proficient at haiku, it seems easiest to describe the process through firsthand experience. I am in the garden weeding. The sun is hot and I am not particularly happy. A butterfly lands on a leaf next to me. I think it is beautiful. It reminds me why I have a garden and that I do like taking care of it. I write the following haiku:

> *Pulling weeds,*
> *hot sun. Next to me,*
> *a butterfly lands on a leaf.*

I don't describe my emotions or my thoughts. By creating a precise picture of what I respond to, I give the reader the potential to have that same experience. I step back and let the image do the talking.

Haiku often juxtapose two contradictory thoughts. Sometimes they are two opposing thoughts or feelings within one event, as in the poem above. Others can be two separate events, as in the following haiku by Paul Marion. On the same day of the summer in 1991, there was a hurricane and the attempted overthrow of the president of the Soviet Union. These two events led to a series of haiku entitled "Haiku for Hurricane Coup."

> *The white dish spins-*
> *I keep looking*
> *for the neighbor's cat.*

In another haiku by Paul Marion, he creates a picture that we can see, hear and feel.

> *Rain sings down*
> *the drain.*
> *Wet night/still.*

Another restriction that is often placed on haiku is that they must be about the seasons or nature. In classical Japanese haiku, the seasons were indicated by specific "season words." Many contemporary haiku in both Japan and the West no longer require these indications. Look for moments in your own life to write your haiku about.

Handmade Books for a Healthy Planet/ ©2010 Susan Kapuscinski Gaylord /makingbooks.com

2. Illustrate the haiku:

a. Cut or tear the illustrations from collage paper. The illustrations can be abstract or representational. They can be as brief and concise as the haiku. Colors can help convey the meaning of the poem. Blues and greens are usually thought of as cool, calming colors and suggest sky, water and growing things. Yellow, red and orange are hot colors that suggest strong emotions, heat and fire. If you wish to make representational pictures but are not comfortable with drawing, build them out of simple shapes. Whether your shapes are simple or more complex, try to cut them directly without drawing them first. There is a freshness and simplicity that comes from what the artist Matisse called "drawing with scissors."

b. Place each illustration piece on scrap paper with the side you want to show face down and cover the surface with a thin layer of glue. Go over the edges and onto the scrap paper. Fold the scrap paper in half with the glue on the inside so nothing will stick to it. Place the piece on the page and smooth to help the glue adhere.

Vary the Book

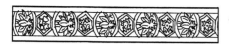

Make a more decorative binding with beads. Use longer thread. Begin the binding on the front of the book and leave a longer tail of thread before you start sewing. After the binding is done and the knot is tied, string beads or buttons on the two ends of thread.

Make a book of leaf rubbings. Collect leaves and insert them into the folded pages. Rub both sides of the paper with the side of a crayon to make prints of both sides of the leaf.

For younger children, use unfolded sheets of paper and a three-hole punch. Use yarn without a needle for sewing. Wrap a little tape around the end of the yarn or dip it in white glue before so it will be easier to sew and won't fray. Clip the book together and push the yarn through the holes. Because the yarn tends to slip off the top and bottom, wrap only the side edges.

Read a Book

Cool Melons—Turn to Frogs!: The Life and Poems of Issa, Matthew Gollub, illustrated by Kazuko G. Stone. New York: Lee & Low Books. Inc., 1998. With elegant illustrations and haiku written in Japanese in the margins, this book tells the story of Issa's life and presents a sampling of the over 20,000 haiku he wrote.

Grass Sandals: The Travels of Basho, Dawnine Spivak, illustrated by Demi. New York: Atheneum Books for Young Readers, 1997. The haiku poet Basho made several journeys on foot throughout Japan. *Grass Sandals* intersperses stories about his travels with his haiku.

In the Eyes of the Cat: Japanese Poetry for All Seasons, selected by Demi. New York: Henry Holt and Company, 1992. This book contains a good selection of haiku and other short poetry from Japan about the seasons.

   Handmade Books for a Healthy Planet/ ©2010 Susan Kapuscinski Gaylord /makingbooks.com

EUROPE

The history of the book in Europe begins in Africa with the papyrus scrolls of Egypt. The use of papyrus as a writing material spread to Greece and Rome where scrolls were the primary book form of the classical era. Our word page comes from the Latin word *pagineum*, which means column on a scroll. The scrolls of Greece and Rome were all writing with no illustrations. One of the largest collections was at the Alexandrian Museum and Library in Alexandria, Egypt. The founding of the library is attributed to Ptolemy II (283–247 BCE). The library housed over 700,000 volumes of works of literature, philosophy and science. Because the scrolls were written by hand, Alexandria became an important city for book production.

Parchment (treated animal skins) came to replace papyrus as a writing surface for books. There is an interesting story about the invention of parchment which may be legend. Around 200 BCE, the Egyptians stopped exporting papyrus. It is said that the Egyptian king was jealous of a new library in Pergamum, Turkey and afraid it might surpass the Alexandrian Library. The librarians at Pergamum looked for a substitute for papyrus and developed parchment. Writing had already been done on leather, but the surface was somewhat rough. The preparation of animal skins into parchment is a more involved process and results in a smooth writing surface.

With the invention of parchment came the evolution of the book from the scroll to the codex. This basic form is the same style of book we use today, with sets of folded sheets gathered and sewn together along the fold. The earliest folded book in existence today is from the second century and is made of papyrus. Folded papyrus books did not hold up well and tended to crack along the folds. Parchment proved to be a more suitable material. Through the sixth century, the papyrus scroll, the papyrus codex and the parchment codex were all used, with the codex form favored by the Christians.

After that time, the parchment codex became the preferred form for everyone. The folded parchment sheets were attached to wooden covers. These were then covered with leather or metalwork.

Because parchment and papyrus were expensive, they were only used for works of lasting value. Accounts, correspondence, and rough drafts were done on wooden tablets that were covered with wax. The writing was scratched into the surface and could be erased when finished. These were used in Greece and Rome and continued to be used in Europe through the Middle Ages. The Greeks also wrote notes on *ostraca* which were pieces of broken pottery.

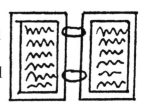

As Christianity spread throughout Europe, the parchment codex traveled with it. Every monastery had a *scriptorium* where monks copied the Bible and the teachings of the early church. Latin was the common language. The writing was often embellished with decorated initial letters and borders. Books were also made for the courts of kings and princes. While the monks were writing on parchment in scriptoria, the Vikings were making their way through Europe and leaving their mark on stones with a form of writing called *runes*. In the twelfth century, book production became more widespread. Scribes and illuminators formed craft guilds and worked on commission for the new merchant class as well as the nobility.

As the demand for books continued to increase, production by hand could not provide a sufficient supply. The earliest printed books in Europe were done with woodcuts, which were originally developed by the Chinese. Text and illustrations were carved into wooden blocks in reverse, one block per page, inked and then printed. Johann Gutenberg invented movable metal type in Europe and produced the first printed Bible in 1455. The first copies were done on parchment, with colored initials and borders added by hand. His idea was to make a book that looked like a handmade one. As printing replaced handwritten books and paper replaced parchment, new styles of lettering and page design developed. The history of books in Europe continued with innovations in type and paper and the mechanical processes of printing and binding.

RUNE STONE

SCANDINAVIA

Left: Stone for Taran, a character in Lloyd Alexander's Book of Three. *Stone made from front panel of grocery bag cut in half with both pieces glued together. / Center: My name written with waterproof black marker on stone. / Right: Stone for Wilbur from* Charlotte's Web. *Stone made from US Letter/ A4 recycled paper folded in half and glued together.*

The Vikings wrote in a kind of writing called runes. The lines were always vertical and diagonal because runes were carved in stone or wood. Curved lines were hard to make and horizontal lines wouldn't show up against the grain of the wood. Rune stones were usually memorial stones for the dead, but occasionally announced the accomplishments of the living. The memorial stones served two purposes: to pay tribute to the dead and as public notice that the death had occurred, rather like an obituary in the newspaper.

Make a paper rune stone as a memorial for a family member or pet or as a tribute to a friend, character in a book or movie, or admired contemporary or historical figure. There is a chart to help you write in runes on page 110. You can write on both sides of the stone, with runes on the front and the translation on the back. If you want your rune stone to stand up, you can attach a support to the back. You can also write in runes with a waterproof marker on a stone gathered from outside.

You'll Need:

- 2 pieces of used paper with writing on one side or front or back panel of grocery bag cut in half

- 1 cereal box side panel with top or bottom flap for stand (optional)

- Glue stick and scrap paper

- Scissors

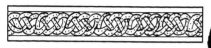 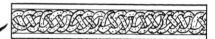

1. Make the stone:

a. Glue the two pieces of paper together with the writing sides facing each other.

b. Cut the paper into a stone shape. The paper can be held horizontally or vertically. The bottom of the stone should be flat.

2. Make the support (optional):

a. Use the width of your hand as a measuring guide. Place your hand next to the flap at one end of the side panel of a cereal box and make a pencil mark on the other side of your hand. Cut the side panel at the line.

b. Starting at the fold at the bottom of the flap, cut the panel on a slight diagonal.

c. Glue or tape the flap to the back of the stone at the bottom in the middle.

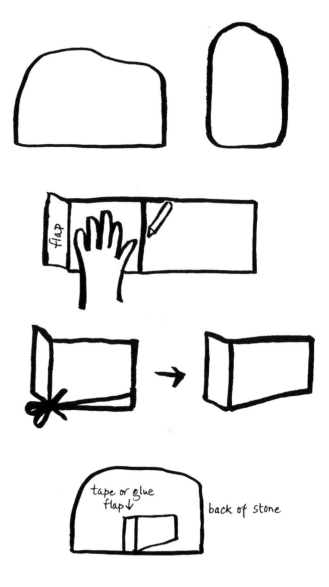

 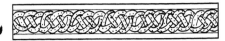

Write your text on a piece of paper (recycled of course). The usual wording was something like this: _____ made this stone for (or in memory of) _____ followed by a description of the person's accomplishments or character. Make a stone for a family member, friend or pet; famous people, living or dead; or characters from books and movies.

Use the Rune Alphabet chart on the following page to turn it into runes. I think it's easiest to write the rune translation on the piece of paper first and then write it on the stone. The runes were usually written between single or double lines. I like to make the lines first, then do the writing in between. There were no spaces between words. A dot or a line indicated the end of one word and the beginning of the next.

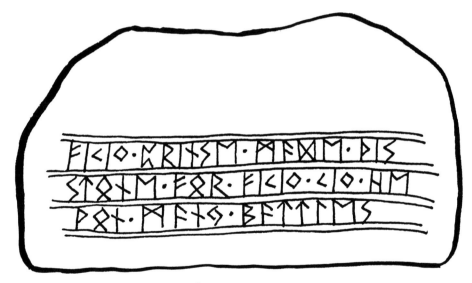

This stone says:
"Viking Prince made this stone for Viking King. He won many battles."

Rune Alphabet

A	B	C	D	E	F	G	H	I	J
F	B	USE RUNE FOR S or K	⋈	M	F	X	N	I	5

K	L	M	N	O	P	Q	R	S	T
<	Γ	M	✝	◇	Ͳ	USE RUNES FOR E+K+S	R	5	↑

U	V	W	X	Y	Z	TH	NG		
Ⴖ	F	Ͼ	USE RUNES FOR K+W	5	Ψ	Þ	◇		

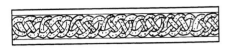 # Vary the Book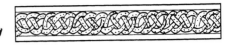

If you are using a stand, cover it with paper on both sides for a more finished look.

Runes were also written on twigs and slats of wood. Some runes showed ownership. A merchant would carry wooden strips in which his name was carved. He would use them as labels by tying them to the goods he intended to buy. Some rune sticks were used to send messages. Use cleaned popsicle sticks. Write runes on the stick with a ball point pen that has run out of ink. Press hard to go into the surface of the stick. Rub over the stick with the side of a brown crayon. Write your name or send a message to a friend.

Runes were also found on thin gold discs that were derived from Roman coins. The discs, called *bracteates*, were stamped with designs and, in some cases, runes. Used as pendants or ornaments, they were sometimes worn for good luck. Cut circles from cereal boxes or use the lids from frozen juice containers and cover them with yellow or gold paper. Write your name and a good luck message in runes.

 # Read a Book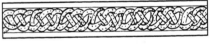

Elfwyn's Saga, David Wisniewski. New York: Lothrop, Lee and Shephard Books, 1990. Elfwyn, born blind because of a curse carved in runes, saves her people from the greedy Gorm and receives her sight.

East of the Sun and West of the Moon, Mercer Mayer. New York: Macmillan Publishing Company, 1980. In this retelling of a Norwegian folktale, a maiden rejects a frog who turns out to be a prince and then rescues him from a troll princess with the help of the Moon, Father Forest, Great Fish of the Sea, and the North Wind. The illustrations include the home of the North Wind which is covered with rune carvings.

PUGILLARE

ANCIENT ROME

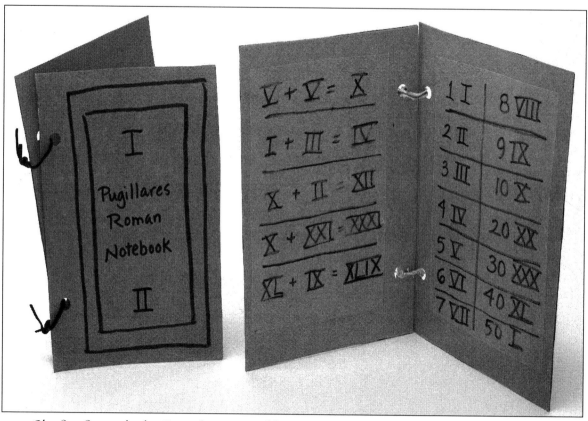

Closed and open books: Pages from a cereal box covered with a brown grocery bag. Ties of twist ties. Waxed paper glued to interior pages.

Handmade Books for a Healthy Planet/ ©2010 Susan Kapuscinski Gaylord /makingbooks.com

Pugillares were notebooks used in ancient Rome. The books were named for the Latin word pugillus *which means "fist" because the books were small enough to be held in the hand. Wooden tablets, tied together with leather cords, were covered with a coating of blackened wax. The writing was done in the wax with a pointed metal stick called a stylus. The notebooks were used for writing rough drafts and correspondence and for figuring accounts. When finished, the wax was smoothed and made ready for fresh writing. Pugillares is a plural Latin word. The singular is pugillare.*

You will use wax paper instead of wax in your *Pugillare*. The book can be a reference guide to Roman numerals and list the numbers and their equivalents in Arabic numerals or it can have math problems in Roman numerals. There is a chart on page 116 to help you. I find waterproof marker works the best.

You'll Need:

- 1 cereal box panel
- Front or back panel of a grocery bag or other brown paper
- Piece of wax paper
- 2 twist ties
- Pencil
- Glue stick and scrap paper
- Scissors

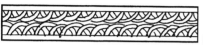 

1. Make the two pages:

a. Place the cereal box panel in front of you so that it is wider than tall. Place your hand on the edge of the panel. Make pencil marks at the side and top of your hand.

b. Using the pencil marks as a guide, draw lines and cut out one page.

c. Place the cut page on a corner of the rest of the cereal box panel. Trace and cut to make the second page.

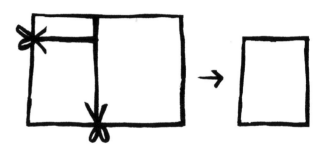

d. Using one of the pages as a pattern, trace and cut four pieces from the grocery bag.

e. Glue a grocery bag piece on the front and back side of each page. Smooth each side with your hand to help the glue adhere.

2. Punch holes and add twist ties:

a. Make two holes along the side of one page.

b. Place the page with the holes on top of the other page. Trace around the inside of the holes. Remove the top page and punch holes in the second page.

c. Cut two pieces of wax paper to fit on the page.

d. Place the two pages on the table so that the hole sides are in the center. Using scrap paper, glue one piece of wax paper on each page.

e. Put the pages together with the wax paper sides facing each other. Thread a twist tie through both pages at each hole. Leave some space before you twist the ties together so that the book will open easily.

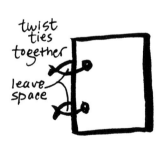

Roman Numerals

I	II	III	IV	V	VI	VII	VIII	IX	X
1	2	3	4	5	6	7	8	9	10

XI	XII	XIII	XIV	XV	XVI	XVII	XVIII	XIX	XX
11	12	13	14	15	16	17	18	19	20

XX	XXX	XL	L	LX	LXX	LXXX	XC	C
20	30	40	50	60	70	80	90	100

CC	CCC	CD	D	DC	DCC	DCCC	CM	M
200	300	400	500	600	700	800	900	1000

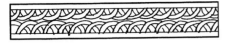 ## Vary the Book

Instead of twist ties from bread, use yarn or pieces cut from plastic bags.

Use the books for correspondence. Use overhead transparency film instead of wax paper and write with overhead markers. Write a message and send the book to a friend. Your friend reads the message, wipes off the marker with a damp paper towel, and writes a return message.

Pugillares often contained more than two pages. Make a book with multiple pages. You can skip the wax paper. Notice that the construction is similar to today's loose-leaf binders. Write stories about the Roman gods and goddesses or ancient Rome.

Read a Book

Roman Numerals I to MM: Numerabilia Romana Uno ad Duo Mila, Arthur Geisert. Boston: Houghton Mifflin Company, 1996. The Roman numerals are explained and illustrated with pictures of pigs. Pages of scenes follow with collections of items to count (I weather vane, XXXVII pigs, II horses).

Daughter of Earth: A Roman Myth, Gerald McDermott. New York: Delacorte Press, 1984. This dramatic retelling of the Roman myth, based on the version in Ovid's *Metamorphoses*, tells the story of Ceres and her daughter Proserpina whose capture by Pluto, god of the Underworld, brings winter to the earth.

Two Roman Mice, by Horace, Marilynne K. Roach. New York: Thomas Y. Crowell Company, 1975. A translation and retelling of Satire II by the Roman poet Quintus Horatius Baccus (Horace) from 65-8 BCE, this is the story of the country mouse and the city mouse. The illustrations combine cute drawings of mice with historical details.

NEWSBOOK

15th AND 16th CENTURY EUROPE

Left: Record of family/personal event. Used US Letter/A4 copy paper pages. Cover of cereal box with newspaper glued on. Elastic binding. / Center: Record of family vacation. Book made from half sheets of used US Letter/A4 copy paper. Cover made by gluing catalog page to front page. Bound with two twist ties. / Right: Newsbook of historical event. Used US Letter/A4 copy paper pages. Cover of cereal box with paper glued on. Elastic binding.

Before newspapers, there were newsbooks. While newspapers tell us all the news of the day, newsbooks, which were also called relations, were about one event. Common topics were explorations and discoveries, wars and natural disasters. The small booklets were illustrated with woodcuts. In 1493, Queen Isabella and King Ferdinand of Spain published the letter they received from Columbus which described his discovery of America. It was translated from Spanish into Latin and German and published in different editions around Europe.

Make a newsbook of an event from history or current events, an event in your life, or write a story about an event in an imaginary place. This binding is one of the simplest to make.

You'll Need:

- 3–4 pieces of used paper with writing on one side only

- 1 cereal box panel

- Elastic

- Scissors

- Pencil

1. Fold each sheet of paper in half the short way like a hamburger with the writing on the inside.

2. Stack the folded pages with the folds on the top. Place the stack on the cereal box panel with a small border on the bottom and a slightly larger border on the side at the edge. Leaving a small border on the top and a larger border on the other side, draw a line around the pages.

3. Cut along the lines. You now have a cover.

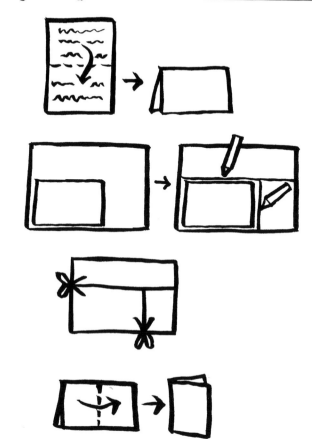

4. Tap the sheets of folded paper together and fold them in half the short way like a hamburger.

5. Fold the cover in half, then open it.

6. Open the pages and place them inside the cover with the fold of the pages on top of the fold of the cover. Insert one side of the pages and cover into an elastic and line up the elastic with the center fold.

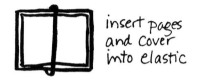

insert pages and cover into elastic

 ## Vary the Book

Use yarn instead of an elastic. Wrap the yarn around the center of the pages and cover and tie a knot at the bottom tightly against the edge of the book. Add beads for decoration if you choose.

For a small book, use two twist ties instead of the elastic. Along the center fold, put one on the inside of the book and one on the outside. Twist them together at top and bottom.

Use the books for a journal or a short story.

 ## Read a Book

Gutenberg, Leonard Everett Fisher. New York: Macmillan Publishing Company, 1993. This picture book gives a little background on printing history, but concentrates on the story of Gutenberg: his experiments with printing and the trials of his business life which included scheming partners and bankruptcies.

Johann Gutenberg and the Amazing Printing Press, Bruce Koscielniak. Boston: Houghton Mifflin Company, 2003. This lively picture book presents lots of information about the process of printing and its development by Gutenberg in a friendly, humorous way.

Pedro's Journal: A Voyage With Christopher Columbus, Pam Conrad, illustrated by Peter Koeppen. Honesdale, PA: Caroline House, 1991. In this chapter book, the story of Columbus' voyage is told through the journal of Pedro de Salcedo, a cabin boy on the Santa Maria.

BOOK OF HOURS

MEDIEVAL EUROPE

Left: Foil cover with "jewels" torn from catalog page. Drawing with waterproof black marker. / Center: Smaller book with pages made from used copy paper folded in half the short way. Cover "jewels" are fruit stickers. / Right: Open book. Illuminated initial outlines are available online.

In medieval times, books were made in monasteries and for royalty and nobility. They were handwritten with a quill or reed and ink on vellum (calfskin) and parchment (sheepskin) and bound between wooden covers. The covers were often covered with leather and sometimes metalwork and jewels. Books of Hours were the bestsellers of the Middle Ages. They contained prayers and devotions to be read throughout the day as well as illustrations and information about each month of the year.

Make a *Book of Hours* about seasonal activities and events during the Middle Ages or today. Your book will have a title page and one page for each month of the year. During the Middle Ages, the first letter of a page or paragraph was often filled in with gold and decorated with designs. These were called illuminated letters. Letters for you to illuminate are in the online supplement.

To imitate the medieval books with metalwork, the cover is covered on the outside with torn pieces of aluminum foil or foil candy wrappers. The inside of the cover is covered with torn pieces of collage paper.

You'll Need:

- 17 sheets of used paper with writing on one side only

- 1 piece of thick thread, twice the paper's height or Short Measure x 2 for US Letter/A4 (See page 9.)

- Piece of aluminum foil or foil candy wrappers

- Collage papers

- Glue stick and scrap paper

- 2 Clothespins

- Push pin and small piece of cardboard

- Tapestry needle, size 16 preferred

- Pencil

- Scissors

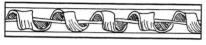 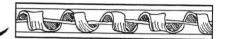

1. Prepare the pages:

a. Place one sheet of paper in front of you so that it is wider than tall and the writing side is facing up.

b. Put a line of glue on either side. Lining up the edges, place another piece of paper on top with the writing side face down. Smooth to help the glue adhere.

c. Repeat seven more times.

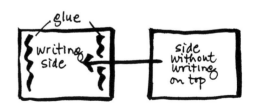

2. Prepare the cover:

The remaining piece of paper is covered with foil on one side (the outside) and torn collage paper on the other. The foil overlaps the edges of the paper to make a more finished looking cover.

a. Using scrap paper, put glue on the non-shiny side of the foil pieces. When you place the foil on the cover paper, have the foil extend a little beyond the edges of the paper and fold it around to the other side. When the entire surface is covered with foil, smooth to help the glue adhere.

b. Do the same with the collage paper on the other side but do not go around the edges.

3. Get ready for sewing:

a. Make a stack of the pages with the cover on the bottom. Tap them together to make the stack even. Fold the stack in half like a hamburger with the cover on the outside.

b. Open the pages. Put one clothespin on the top on one side of the center fold and the other on the bottom on the other side of the fold. The clothespins will stay on the book until you are finished sewing.

c. Make three pencil marks along the center fold for the holes: in the center, one thumb-end from the top, and one thumb-end from the bottom.

d. At each dot, place the piece of cardboard underneath. Place the push pin on the dot and push the pin through to make a hole.

e. Make the holes bigger by pushing the needle into each hole and pulling it through from the other side. If it is hard to get through, wiggle the needle.

f. If the needle has a large eye, tie the thread onto the needle with a double knot to keep it from slipping off. Do not tie a knot at the end. The thread will be used singly.

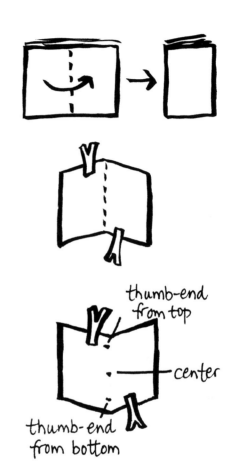

thumb-end from top

center

thumb-end from bottom

double knot

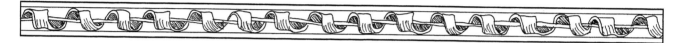

4. Sew the book:

a. Starting from the inside of the book, put the needle into the center hole. Pull the thread through and place the end of the thread under the bottom clothespin.

inside of book

b. Turn the book over to the outside and go into the top hole.

outside of book

c. Turn the book over to the inside. Make a long stitch from the top hole to the bottom hole.

inside of book

d. Turn the book over to the outside and go into the center hole.

outside of book

e. Turn the book over to the inside. Remove the needle. Arrange the thread so that the ends of the thread go out to either side of the long stitch. Gently pull the ends of the thread to make sure the stitches are tight. Tie the two ends in a double knot over the long stitch. If you know how to make a square knot, do so.

inside of book

f. If the ends of the thread are long, trim them so that they are about a thumb-end long. Do not cut any closer to the knot. If you clip the ends too close to the knot, it may unravel.

double knot, square if you can

126

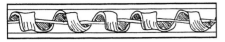 # Vary the Book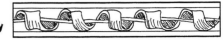

Make a Bestiary or Herbiary. Both books were common in the Middle Ages. Bestiaries contained pictures and descriptions of animals, both real and imaginary. Herbiaries were about plants.

Make the simple folded booklet (*Comic Book*) on page 58 and use it for a Medieval Dictionary with definitions of words like knight, sword and castle.

Make blank books with collage papers on both sides of the cover to use for journals and notebooks.

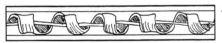 # Read a Book

Marguerite Makes A Book, Bruce Robertson, illustrated by Kathryn Hewitt. Los Angeles: J. Paul Getty Museum, 1999. This beautifully illustrated picture book tells of Marguerite, a girl in medieval Paris. Her father illuminates books and she helps him finish an important commission of a Book of Hours for Lady Isabelle.

Across A Dark and Wild Sea, Don Brown. Brookfield, Ct: Roaring Brook Press, 2002. The Irish monk Columcille's love of books and skill as a scribe led to a fierce battle. Regretting the blood shed, the monk exiled himself to the barren island of Iona off the rocky coast of Scotland. His settlement grew to a monastery which helped to preserve learning and the making of books during the dark ages.

Bibles and Bestiaries: A Guide to Illuminated Manuscripts, Elizabeth B. Wilson. New York: Farrar, Straus and Giroux, 1994. Clearly written and illustrated with examples from manuscripts in the Pierpont Morgan Library in New York, the book includes a detailed description of the process of creating an illuminated manuscript from making the vellum to binding the book.

 # Bibliography

Asihene, Emmanuel V., *Understanding the Traditional Art of Ghana*. Rutherford, New Jersey: Fairleigh Dickinson University Press, 1978.

Barker, Nicolas, *Treasures of the British Library*. New York: Harry N. Abrams, Inc., 1988.

Brookfield, Karen, *Book*. New York: Alfred A. Knopf, 1993.

Brulliard, Karin, "Revived interest in old books could restore Timbuktu's glory", *The Boston Globe*, January 10, 2010.

Diringer, David, *The Book Before Printing: Ancient, Medieval and Oriental*. New York: Dover Publications, 1982.

Emmerich, André, *Art Before Columbus*. New York: Simon & Schuster, 1963.

Gaur, Albertine, *A History of Writing*. New York: Cross River Press, 1992.

Guar, Albertine, *Writing Materials of the East*. London: The British Library, 1979.

Guojun, Liu and Zheng Rusi, *The Story of Chinese Books*. Beijing: Foreign Languages Press: 1985.

Henry, David J., *Beyond Words: The Art of the Book*. Rochester, New York: Memorial Art Gallery, University of Rochester, 1986.

Higginson, William J., *The Haiku Handbook: How To Write, Share, and Teach Haiku*. New York: McGraw-Hill, 1989.

Jackson, Donald, *The Story of Writing*. New York: Taplinger Publishing Co., Inc, 1981.

Jolles, Frank, "Traditional Zulu Beadwork of the Msinga Area." *African Arts*, vol. 25, no. 1, (January 1993) pp. 42-53.

Mack, John, ed., *Ethnic Jewelry*, New York, Harry N. Abrams, Inc., 1988.

Martinique, Edward, *Chinese Traditional Bookbinding: A Study of Its Evolution and Techniques*, Republic of China: Chinese Materials Center, 1983.

McMurtrie, Douglas C., *The Book: The Story of Printing and Bookmaking*, New York, Dorset Press, 1943.

Mercier, Jacques, *Ethiopian Magic Scrolls*. New York: George Braziller, 1979.

Page, R. I., *Runes: Reading the Past*. Berkeley, California: University of California Press, 1987.

Quarcoo, A. K., *The Language of Adinkra Patterns*. Legon, Ghana: Institute of African Studies, University of Ghana, 1972.

Sayer, Chloe, *Arts and Crafts of Mexico*. San Francisco: Chronicle Books, 1990.

Schuman, Jo Miles, *Art from Many Hands: Multicultural Art Projects*. Worcester, Massachusetts: Davis Publications, Inc, 1981.

Steffens, Bradley, *Printing Press: Ideas in Type*. San Diego: Lucent Books, 1990.

Tsien, Tsuen-Hsuin, *Written on Bamboo and Silk*. Chicago: University of Chicago Press, 1962.

Ullman, B. L., *Ancient Writing and Its Influence*. Toronto: University of Toronto Press, 1980.

Handmade Books for a Healthy Planet

ONLINE

makingbooks.com/hbhp

Show and Tell
Color photos and video of all the sample books

Video of authentic books from around the world from my collection

Bookmaking Help
Line guides and patterns for making your books

Video instructions on *The Basics*

Web Explorations
Links to accompany each project

Recycling Information

Links for more information on making handmade books

Handmade Books for a Healthy Planet/ ©2010 Susan Kapuscinski Gaylord /makingbooks.com